ETHNIC CHRONOLOGY SERIES
NUMBER 16

The Koreans in America
1882-1974
A Chronology & Fact Book

Compiled and edited by

Hyung-chan Kim
and
Wayne Patterson

1974
OCEANA PUBLICATIONS, INC.
DOBBS FERRY, NEW YORK

Library of Congress Cataloging in Publication Data

Kim, Hyung-chan.
  The Koreans in America, 1882-1974.

  (Ethnic chronology series, no. 16)
  Bibliography: p.
  1. Koreans in the United States--History. I. Pat-
terson, Wayne, joint author. II. Title. III. Series.
E184.K6K48   917.3'06'957   74-13732
ISBN 0-379-00513-1

Manufactured in the United States of America.

TABLE OF CONTENTS

iv

As early as 1883, the Korean diplomatic mission led by the queen's nephew, Min Young-ik, came to visit the United States to learn from its economic, educational, industrial, and political institutions, advanced knowledge to be applied in the efforts to modernize Korea. One of the members of the mission, Yu Kil-jun, decided to remain in America to study at the Dammer Academy in Massachusetts. Upon his return to Korea he wrote a book, Soyu Kyonmun, (What I Saw and Heard during My Visit to the West), which introduced, for the first time in the long history of Korea, her people to the complex civilization of the West. It was not until January 1903, however, that a large number of Korean emigrants came to the Hawaiian Islands as laborers for the Hawaiian sugar plantations. Many of them were farmers unable to eke out a living from their rice paddies scorched by a severe drought, ex-soldiers who had resisted without success the Japanese military infiltration into their fatherland, and displaced individuals who had lost their property during the Sino-Japanese War. With the encouragement from their government and American missionaries, they responded to the recruitment effort of agents who had been dispatched to Korea by a number of overseas development companies. The first group of Korean emigrants aboard the S.S. Gaelic arrived at Honolulu on January 13, 1903, and the emigration of Koreans to the Hawaiian Islands continued until 1905, when the Korean government decided to put an end to the emigration of its subjects under political pressure from Imperial Japan. Although the Korean emigrants came from different parts of the Korean peninsula and from different walks of life, they shared with each other a common cause in their struggle for national independence.

During the short period between 1903 and 1905, a total of 7,226 Koreans came to the Hawaiian Islands, and they began to transplant their culture in an alien environment immediately after their arrival. One of the first aspects of Korean culture transplanted in the Hawaiian Islands was the Dong-hoi, or the village council, a traditional Korean political organization for self-government. As there arose the need for law and order among the Korean emigrants, they organized the village councils at various work camps occupied by the Korean laborers who were punished by the Dong-chang, or the head of the village council, when they were found unruly and disorderly. Secondly, a number of sworn brotherhood organizations and clan associations were established by Koreans who felt a strong need for collective succor and support in an alien culture. Thirdly, efforts were made to establish the Korean church by the people who had been converted to Christianity prior to their departure from Korea for their new land of adventure and adversity. The first church service was held on a sugar plantation at Mokuleia, on the Island of Oahu on July 4, 1903. Once the church was well established in the Korean community in the Hawaiian Islands and the Mainland of the United States, it became an indispensable instrument for maintenance and perpetuation of Korean culture and for the

Korean national independence movement, which was directed in the United States by the Korean National Association established on February 1, 1909. Korean language schools were established within local churches in order to teach children Korean culture, history, and language.

The strong cohesive force among the Koreans from the beginning of their life in the United States was the goal of liberating their nation from Japanese control. Many a leader emerged from the Korean American community to lead the Korean national independence movement. This political imperative, however, became also a divisive force among the Koreans who were divided over the direction and methods of the independence movement. In order to buttress their individual positions on the movement, its leaders established their own organizations. Ahn Ch'ang-ho was instrumental in establishing the Hungsa-dan, or the Corps for the Advancement of Individuals, while Syngman Rhee was responsible for the establishment of the Dongji-hoi, or the Comrade Society. Pak Yong-man opposed Syngman Rhee, who believed that diplomacy should be a major weapon in the effort to bring about Korea's independence from Imperial Japan. Pak believed strongly that Koreans needed to build a strong military force to fight against Japan if Koreans wanted to free their nation from Japanese control. Because of this belief, Pak established the Kun-dan, or the Military Corps. Korea's freedom from Imperial Japan, however, did not come either from a well orchestrated diplomacy as advocated by Syngman Rhee, or from a military confrontation with Japan as asserted by Pak Yong-man; it came from a combination of historical forces over which Koreans in the United States did not have any control.

The Korean American community, established by the original emigrants, is now being numerically strengthened by new waves of immigrants from Korea, which has sent more than 100,000 of its people to the United States since 1968. During the one year period between July 1972 and June 1973 alone, a total of 22,930 Koreans emigrated to the United States. This constitutes the third largest national group of all other immigrants who came to the United States from various parts of the world during the period. The new influx of Korean emigrants has put the Korean American community in a state of flux, and it is extremely difficult, if not impossible, to forecast what kinds of basic changes will be brought to the Korean American community by the changed conditions in the social demography and political culture of Koreans in America. Nevertheless, it is abundantly clear that the new waves of Korean immigrants in America will certainly have social and political impact upon their host country in general, and upon the Korean American community in particular in the years to come.

The present chronology is an attempt to provide readers with information which will increase their basic understanding of the persons and events that have left a lasting influence upon the development of the history of Koreans in America. Therefore, it is not meant to be exhaustive. The documents attached here are basically from two different sources. First, the editor made an attempt to provide readers with documents relating to the people who had been responsible for the emigration of Koreans to America. Second, the editor selected documents which had been written by Korean immigrants, the majority of whom were first-generation Koreans.

Two major works previously published in Korean have been used as references for this book. The first is Kim Won-yong's Chae-Mi Hanin O-simnyonsa, or the Fifty Year History of Koreans in America, and the second is Noh Jae-yon's Chae-Mi Hanin Yaksa, or a Concise History of Ko-·reans in America, which is a two-volume work. Other minor works used as references are Suh Kwang-woon's Miju Hanin Ch'ilsimnyon-sa, or the Seventy Year History of Koreans in America, Yun Yo-jon's Miju Imin Ch'ilsimnyon, or the Immigration to America for Seventy Years, and Hae-bang Choson, or the Liberated Korea, published by the United Korean Committee. The following unpublished works have been used as references extensively: Kyung Sook Cho Gregor, "Korean Immigrants in Gresham, Oregon: Community Life and Social Adjustment"; Sister Deborah Church, "Korean Emigration to Hawaii: An Aspect of U.S. - Japanese Relations"; Helen Lewis Givens, "The Korean Community in Los Angeles County"; Kingsley K. Lyu, "Korean Nationalist Activities in Hawaii and America, 1901-1945"; Kyung Lee, "Settlement Patterns of Los Angeles Koreans"; and Jai Kun Yoo, "The Koreans in the United States: A Seattle Study." A bibliographical guide to the existing literature on the topic of Koreans in America is appended at the end of this work.

The editor is indebted to many persons who have spurred him on to complete this work. My thanks go to Professor Jesse Hiraoka, Dean of the College of Ethnic Studies, Western Washington State College, who has shown a deep interest in this work. I am grateful to Professor Dae-sook Suh, Director of the Korean Research Center, University of Hawaii, who made various research facilities of the center available to the editor during the summer of 1973. My colleague, Mr. Wayne Patterson, has given me an invaluable assistance at various stages of the compilation of the book. But for his personal and professional interest in the book, it would not have been completed. My thanks also go to Miss Candyce Kaku who typed a major portion of the manuscript with patience and understanding. I am grateful to Mrs. Jane Clark and Mrs. Helen Moran of Western Washington State College for typing the final draft. My wife, Seung-joo, and my daughter, Kathryn, have spent many days and weekends without me while I was away from them physically and often mentally to make this book possible. The sacrifice they have made to see through the compilation of this book is deeply appreciated.

Hyung-chan Kim
College of Ethnic Studies
Western Washington State College
Bellingham, Washington

1882   May 22. The Treaty of Amity and Commerce was signed
              between the United States and Korea. The treaty had a pro-
              viso pertaining to the emigration of Koreans to the United
              States of American proper. Article VI of the treaty stated:
              "Subjects of Chosen (Korea) who may visit the United States
              shall be permitted to reside and to rent premises, purchase
              land, or to construct residences or warehouses in all parts
              of the country...."

1883   September 2. The Korean diplomatic mission led by Min
              Young-ik arrived in San Francisco. During their short visit
              in America the members of the Korean mission visited a
              number of key cultural, industrial, and political establish-
              ments in an attempt to learn as much as they could from
              America. A member of the mission, Yu Kil-jun decided
              to stay in America to study. It was reported that Yu Kil-
              jun entered the Dammer Academy in the state of Massachu-
              setts.

1884   Suh Jae-p'il came to America after his attempt to reform
              Korea had failed in 1884. He changed his name, when he
              was naturalized, to Philip Jaisohn.

              So Kwang-bom and P'yon Su came to America after their at-
              tempt to reform the Korean government had failed in 1884.
              P'yon was killed in a railroad accident while working for
              the United States Agriculture Department in 1891. So
              Kwang-bom returned to Korea as minister of justice and he
              was later appointed as Korean envoy extraordianary and
              minister plenipotentiary to Washington in 1896. He was re-
              placed in the fall of that year. He purchased a house in
              Washington, D.C. with $4,500 which he took from the le-
              gation funds. He died in Washington, D.C. on August 13,
              1897.

1896   November 2. During the meeting of the executive council
              of the Board of Immigration, a Mr. Grunwaldt's proposal
              to import Koreans into the Hawaiian Islands to substitute
              for Chinese and Japanese agricultural laborers was dis-
              cussed. The council did not take any action with exception
              of passing a resolution that read: "Resolved, that the gov-
              ernment look favorably upon the proposition to import Ko-
              rean laborers, but will await applications from the Planters,
              that the government will assume no further responsibility
              than simply consenting to grant permits upon the same terms
              for which permits are granted for Chinese and Japanese."

1897   August 27. During the meeting of the executive council of
        the Board of Immigration, the application submitted by H.
        Hackfeld Company to import Korean lagorers under contract
        was denied. No reasons were mentioned in the minutes of
        the council.

1898   May 11. Pack Jang-hing, a merchant, boarded the China at
        Yokohama, Japan and arrived in Honolulu for business and
        trade on May 20.

1900   January 8. Kam Chung-yu and Leong Pak-hung, whose oc-
        cupations were listed as druggist and laborer, respectively,
        arrived in Honolulu.

        January 12. The S.S. Doric brought Chin Sing-kik, Hung
        Sing-yai, and Hung Wing-tuck to Honolulu.

1901   January 9. The Bureau of Immigration recorded the first
        Korean immigrant as Peter Ryu, who arrived in Hawaii via
        a Japanese ship, Hongkong Maru.

        Five Korean laborers were imported to Hawaii for the year
        ending June 30, 1901. One of them was Chang Sung-pong,
        who worked for the circuit court and police department in
        Honolulu as an interpreter until his death in 1949.

1902   The Hawaii Sugar Planters Association sent David W. Desh-
        ler to Korea to recruit Korean laborers.

        Twelve male Koreans were imported to Hawaii for the year
        ending June 30, 1902.

        The Emperor of Korea granted permission to D.W. Deshler,
        and American citizen, to control Korean laborers to be em-
        ployed abroad.

        December 22. The first group of Korean emigrants aboard
        the S.S. Gaelic left Chemulp'o, now Inch'on, for Hawaii.

1903   January 13. One hundred and two Korean immigrants aboard
        the S.S. Gaelic arrived in Honolulu, Hawaii. They were in-
        spected on board the vessel instead of at Quarantine Island,
        which was the customary inspection station. Collector
        Stackable, when asked to explain, refused to give a reason
        for the change. In this group of the first Korean immigrants
        there were fifty-six men, twenty women, and twenty-five

children. After a few days of rest and recuperation, they were sent to the Waialua Plantation on the Island of Oahu.

March 3. A total of fifty-nine men and one woman arrived in Honolulu via the Coptic and they were sent to the Koloa Plantation on the Island of Oahu.

March 19. A total of seventy-two Koreans arrived in Honolulu aboard the Korea.

April 30. A group of 113 Korean immigrants arrived in Honolulu aboard the Japan. Because of a misunderstanding between Kang Dae-geun, an interpreter for the Korean group, and the immigration officials, they were detained until May 6, when they were released to go to a plantation on the Island of Hawaii.

Frederick V. Berger filed suit against E. Faxon Bishop who was accused by Berger of being responsible for solicitation, encouragement, and prepayment of transportation costs for 113 alien Koreans who arrived in Honolulu aboard the Nippon Maru on April 30. Berger hoped to make $113,000, as he would be entitled to $1,000 for each violation of the immigration law passed by Congress on March 3, 1903, if he had succeeded in proving that such violation was committed by Bishop, who represented sugar planters in Hawaii.

The Pacific Commercial Advertiser reported that a manager of a local agricultural company was satisfied with the performance of Korean laborers: "Manager John Sherman of the Hawaiian Agricultural Co., Pahala, is very pleased with the Koreans as field laborers. He has built them new quarters and they seem contented. The laborers' quarters in general at Pahala have been overhauled, to their betterment in comfort and hygiene."

Choi Dong-soon worked for Frederick V. Berger to bribe a Korean immigrant who would testify in court that he came to Hawaii as a contract laborer. The plot was discovered when Choi was arrested and fined $100 for practicing medicine without a proper license.

July 4. The first church service among the Korean immigrants was held at Mokuleia on the Island of Oahu. The service was led by Kim E-je. Among the Korean immigrants who came to Hawaii between 1903 and 1905, there were approximately 400 Christians and as many as 30 among them were engaged in evangelical work prior to their departure from their mother country.

August 7. Hong Seung-ha, Ahn Jong-su, Yun Byong-gu and others established the New People's Association. Han Ju-dong became chairman of the association. This was the first social and political organization of Koreans in the United States proper. The purpose of the organization was to bring unity among Korean people for their country's independence.

September 23. A total of nine Koreans in San Francisco met at a local Chinese residence and established a Friend-ship Association. Ahn Ch'ang-ho was elected president.

September 29. The United States District Court in Honolulu rendered judgement in favor of defendant Bishop with plain-tiff Berger taking nothing. The court held that since the vi-olation occurred prior to March 3, 1903, the date of pass-age of the act, Berger was in no position to assert that the defendant violated the immigration law of March 3, 1903.

Pak Yun-sop was hired as an interpreter and inspector by the U.S. Bureau of Immigration. Although Pak did not speak English, he spoke Japanese. His wife understood basic English.

1904   February 17. A.W. Taylor, a former employee at the Un-san Mine in Korea, made an attempt to collect passage fees from Korean immigrants. He visited a plantation on the Island of Oahu to collect passage fees. A group of Koreans were infuriated by his attitude and gave him a beating. As a consequence of this incident, eight Koreans were prose-cuted and given a three-month imprisonment.

March 2. A group of Korean Christians rented a house lo-cated on Emma School Street and moved the Korean Evan-gelical Society to the new place.

June 1. The Coptic brought a group of 130 Koreans to Hono-lulu.

July 8. The Mongolia arrived in Honolulu with a group of 176 Koreans.

July 30. A group of ninety Korean immigrants arrived in
Honolulu.

A group of 154 Korean immigrants arrived in Honolulu on
the Coptic. One of them died of a disease, which prompted
the authorities to detain passengers for a period of twelve
days.

September 26. The Mongolia brought to Honolulu a group
of 152 Korean immigrants.

November 29. Syngman Rhee arrived in Honolulu aboard
the Siberia. He left Honolulu to arrive in San Francisco on
December 4. Later he went to Washington, D.C. in order
to enter George Washington University.

December 8. Japanese laborers went on strike at the Waialua plantation on the Island of Oahu. A number of police
officials were dispatched to the place of labor dispute and
250 Korean laborers were recruited from various places to
work at the plantation.

1905   February 6. Pak Yong-man, an important figure in the Korean national independence movement, arrived in San Francisco.

February 10. A ceremony establishing the Korean Episcopal Church was held at the St. Andrew Church in Honolulu,
and the church rented a school classroom for church services in April. In October of the same year, the church began to use a part of a Chinese Episcopal church building.
In January 1925, the members of the church made a total of
$1,800 towards the construction of a church building, and
in May, a building was completed to house the Korean Episcopal Church. This building was used until 1952. In 1952,
the church building was expanded at a cost of $62,327, and
a ceremony dedicating the church building was held on July
13, 1952. This is the present church building of the Korean
Episcopal Church. The church also held Korean language
classes for children in order to educate second-generation
Koreans.

The number of Koreans going to the mainland to work on
the railroad to connect Seattle, Washington with St. Paul,
Minnesota gradually increased as the office responsible for
recruiting laborers for railroad work was established within the Hansung Hotel operated by a Korean, Mun Hong-sok.

March 31. A group of 276 Korean immigrants arrived in Honolulu aboard the Manchuria.

April 5. The Friendship Association established in 1903 in San Francisco expanded its work and changed its name to the Mutual Cooperation Federation. Ahn Ch'ang-ho became its president and traveled to Riverside and Redlands for an observation tour.

A group of 191 Korean immigrants arrived in Honolulu aboard the Korea.

April 30. The first Korean church building was dedicated at the Ewa plantation on Oahu. A total of 110 people attended the dedication ceremony. Rev. John Wadman of Honolulu also attended the ceremonial occasion.

May 3. The Chinmok-hoi of Ewa, or the Friendship Society of Ewa, Oahu was organized under the initiative of Chong Myong-won, Kim Song-kwon, Yun Byong-gu, Yi Man-ch'un, Kim Kyi-sop and Kang Yong-so. The purpose of the Friendshop Society was to launch an anti-Japanese movement, to refuse Japanese goods, and to love compatriots. The name of the society was changed to Chunghung-hoi or Forward Prosperity Society in 1906.

May 18. A group of 288 Korean immigrants arrived in Honolulu aboard the Mongolia.

The Hanin Sisa, or the Korean News, was published between June 10, 1905 and September, 1906 in Honolulu. This semimonthly publication was mainly supported by members of the Methodist Church of Honolulu and contributed to the elimination of illiteracy among Koreans.

July 9. A Korean Methodist church was officially established in Honolulu and the dedication service was held with the Rev. John Wadman and the Rev. Yun Byong-gu attending.

A number of Korean residents in the San Francisco area organized the Korean Evangelical Society and conducted church services with the assistance of Mun Kyong-ho. Beginning on July 15, 1906, the evangelist Bang Wha-jung conducted church services. This was the beginning of the Korean Methodist Church of San Francisco. After Evangelist Yang Ju-sam was elected to conduct church services, the Korean

Evangelical Society rented a house at 2350 California Street
and held a ceremony dedicating the church building on December 16, 1906. On August 5, 1911, the Rev. Yi Dae-wi
was assigned to the pastoral duty and the society was
changed to the Korean Methodist Church. In June 1928,
members of the church contributed toward the construction
of a church building and later completed the construction
with financial assistance from the Methodist Episcopal Mission South. The building was completed at a cost of $18,000.
The church began to publish its newsletter, the Korean Federation Church Bulletin on July 13, 1907. Yang Ju-sam,
Yun Byong-gu and Yi Dae-wi served as editors.

August 13. The Rev. John Wadman attended the dedication
ceremony of a Korean church building.

The Rev. Yun Byong-gu was chosen as the representative
of the 7,000 Korean immigrants in Hawaii to be sent to the
mainland to present the case of Korea before President
Theodore Roosevelt, who arranged a meeting between Russia and Japan. The Rev. Yun obtained from Secretary of
War Taft a letter of introduction to President Roosevelt
and left Hawaii on the Alameda. He went to George Washington University to accompany Syngman Rhee to see the president. They went to see Rossevelt in New York in the early
part of August, who told them that such an important matter
should be submitted to him through official government chan-
nels. The Reverend Yun returned to Hawaii on October 17
without any results accomplished toward the mission for
which he had been sent.

August 24. The Korean People's Mutual Assistance Society
was established according to the suggestions made by the
Rev. John Wadman. Song Hon-joo was elected chairman.
One dollar per person was charged as membership fee and
every member was to pay fifty cents once every three
months.

September 8. Aboard the Manchuria, Yun Ch'i-ho, an official from the Korean Foreign Office, arrived in Honolulu.
He was on his way to Mexico to investigate the living conditions facing Korean immigrants in Mexico.

Song Sok-jun arrived in Hawaii on his way from Korea to
San Francisco in the early part of September. Later he became the editor of the Mutual Cooperation News.

September 18. The Reverend Noble who spent years in Korea as a missionary, arrived in Honolulu and visited many Korean churches.

September 22. The Mutual Cooperation Federation established in San Francisco began to publish its own newspaper. Song Sok-jun became its editor.

In October, at Hanapepe, on the Island of Kauai, Chakanghoi, or the Self-strengthening Society, was organized. Song Kon was elected president of the society, the purpose of which was to promote education and knowledge. The society published its Chakang Monthly which was then published at the store of Yi Hong-ki at Hanapepe. The editor of the monthly was Ko Sok-ju.

The Mutual Cooperation Federation established in San Francisco expanded as more Koreans moved to San Francisco from Hawaii. The ceremony dedicating the federation's headquarters building was held on November 14. The headquarters was established at 938 Pacific Street.

The Korean Methodist Church of Hawaii began to publish its Honolulu Korean Church Bulletin in November. The monthly published sermons as well as Bible lessons in order to encourage Bible study among Koreans in Hawaii. The name of the bulletin was changed to the Korean Church Bulletin in April 1914, and continued to publish its Bible lessons until October 1940.

November 4. Twenty-two Koreans left Honolulu for the Mainland aboard the Mongolia.

November 12. A Korean left Honolulu for the Mainland aboard the China.

November 16. Six Koreans left Honolulu for the Mainland aboard the Siberia.

November 20. Six Koreans arrived in San Francisco aboard the Seattle.

A local citizens' meeting was held at a community hall located on Mission Street in San Francisco, and the citizens passed a resolution opposing the entrance of the Japanese and Koreans. The resolution was then sent to the U.S. Congress.

December 3. News from Seoul reported that the American minister to Korea, Edwin V. Morgan, withdrew the U.S. legation from Korea.

December 5. Eight Koreans left Honolulu for San Francisco aboard the Manchuria.

December 9. The Great Unity Education Association was established in Pasadena, and Kim U-je was elected president of the association. The association's name was changed to the Great Unity Fatherland Protection Association in January 1907. It established a number of branch offices and elected Lee Byong-ho as its president.

December 17. A group of twenty-two Koreans left Honolulu for San Francisco aboard the Korea.

December 21. Min Yong-ch'an, Korean minister to France, arrived in Washington to make a plea for American support in annulling the Protectorate Treaty signed between Japan and Korea. Having failed to achieve his mission, he returned to Paris.

December 26. The Mutual Cooperation Federation established its branch office in Redlands.

December 28. The annual meeting of the Korean Methodist church was held at a local Methodist church in Honolulu. The Reverend Hamilton presided over the meeting, which was the first Korean Methodist church meeting. It took three days to complete its business. A total of thirteen Korean ministers were appointed to various local Korean churches.

1906   January 9. A group of five Koreans left Honolulu for San Francisco aboard the Alameda.

January 12. A group of four Koreans left Honolulu for San Francisco aboard the Siberia.

February 6. As a result of the Russo-Japanese Treaty, the Korean legation in Washington was withdrawn and Acting Minister Kim Yun-jong left San Francisco aboard the Mongolia.

February 8. A group of tweleve Koreans arrived in San Francisco from Honolulu aboard the Manchuria.

February 12. A Wesley home was dedicated in Honolulu. The ceremony was officiated by the Reverend Hamilton. The purpose of the Wesley home was to accommodate orphans and widows of both Japanese and Korean nationalities.

March 16. The Mutual Cooperation Federation established its branch office in Los Angeles.

March 29. A group of twenty-two Koreans arrived in San Francisco from Honolulu aboard the Manchuria.

April 6. Mr. Thurston, a member of the Honolulu Social Science Club, presented a report on the number of immigrants by their nationality. According to his report, there were 6,908 Korean immigrants as of 1905.

April 12. A group of nineteen Koreans arrived in San Francisco from Honolulu aboard the Sonoma.

April 18. The headquarters building of the Mutual Cooperation Federation was burned down during the San Francisco earthquake, but no persons of Korean ancestry were hurt or killed by the earthquake. The Daily Newspaper, in Seoul, Korea, sent $592,23 to help Koreans suffering from the disaster.

The king of Korea sent a sum of $1,900 to help Koreans who suffered financial loss. The money was distributed to Koreans by the Reverend Moffett, a former missionary who worked with Horace Allen. The Mutual Cooperation Federation received financial assistance and reestablished its headquarters, which was moved to Oakland, California.

May 4. It is reported that the Korean Methodist church in Honolulu published its first church monthly report by means of a printing machine. Previously, the monthly report had been mimeographed. The printed church monthly report was distributed among thirty-six Korean churches located in the islands.

May 10. A group of Korean residents in Los Angeles established a Presbyterian mission with the assistance of the Presbyterian Missionary Extension Board. The mission was later promoted to the status of church on April 9, 1921, and the Reverend Kim Jung-soo was assigned to the church in 1929. On February 16, 1937, the Reverend Kim Sung-nak

became pastor of the church. In November of the same
year, a lot was purchased on West Jefferson Boulevard and
a building was constructed at a cost of $22,000.

May 11. The Mutual Cooperation Federation held its council meeting and changed its counselor system into a representative system. At the meeting, Song Sok-jun was elected
head of the Bureau of Education.

Thirty Koreans were recruited for certain work from Honolulu, and they were taken to Seattle during the early weeks
of May.

Mr. Yang Ju-sam arrived in Oakland by way of London and
New York. He was to work with the Korean Methodist
Church of San Francisco.

August 2. A group of thirty Koreans arrived in San Francisco from Honolulu aboard the Manchuria.

August 5. A group of six Koreans arrived in San Francisco
from Honolulu aboard the Alameda.

August 11. It was reported that the Methodist Episcopal
Mission purchased a building at a price of $1,800. The
building was used to house a Korean boarding school and the
headquarters for Korean churches.

The Reverend George Heber Jones, a long time friend of
Koreans, defended Koreans against racist remarks made
by Robinson, a local judge, who had made a public statement to the effect that Puerto Ricans, Portuguese, and Koreans were immoral and religious fanatics.

August 13. The public was invited to the Korean church located on Punchbowl Street for an open house. Also invited
was the Reverend George H. Jones.

The Reverend Jones, who had encouraged Koreans to emigrate to Hawaii, expressed his satisfaction with the progress
Korean immigrants had made since their arrival in Hawaii.

August 14. The Montana brought three Koreans from Honolulu to San Francisco.

August 25. A group of fifty-two Koreans arrived in San
Francisco from Honolulu aboard the Korea.

September 2. The Korean Boarding School was established.
Mrs. Wadman served as principal of the school for a period of seven years. In September of 1913, Syngman Rhee
was appointed principal of the school, the name of which
was changed to the Korean Central Institute.

September 12. A group of twelve Koreans arrived in San
Francisco from Honolulu aboard the China.

October 11. Choi Jong-ik came to San Francisco from Korea.

November 8. A group of fifty-two Koreans arrived in San
Francisco from Honolulu aboard the Korea.

November 11. A Korean church building on Lihue Plantation on the Island of Kauai was dedicated, and the Reverend
Hyon Sun-ryang presided over the dedication ceremony.

November 28. A group of seventy-four Koreans came to
San Francisco from Honolulu aboard the Siberia.

November 29. A group of fifty-nine Koreans arrived in San
Francisco from Honolulu aboard the Korea.

December 2. The Kongjin-hoi, or Mutual Progress Society,
was organized in Honolulu by Min Ch'an-ho, Yi Nae-soo,
Im Jun-ho, and Im Chong-soo. The Purpose of the society
was to train leaders. Min Ch'an-ho was elected president.

December 15. A Korean youth group received an award at
the Kamehameha Memorial Church.

During the early weeks of December, Mr. Pak Je-sun opened
a hotel on Rich Street, Salt Lake City, Utah, and began
to accommodate Korean railroad workers in the vicinity
of Salt Lake City, Utah.

1907   January 1. A youth rally meeting was held at the new Korean church building on Punchbowl Street. Delegates from
the Islands of Kauai, Maui, Hawaii, and Oahu were represented at the meeting, which heard a sermon by the Reverend John Wadman. Later the delegates discussed future
church development.

January 2. A group of sixteen Koreans arrived in San Francisco from Honolulu aboard the Alameda.

January 8. Ahn Ch'ang-ho returend to Korea.

February 4. The Siberia brought from Honolulu to San Francisco a group of ten Koreans, while five on the Alameda and seven on the China arrived from Honolulu to San Francisco on the same day.

February 16. The U.S. Senate passed the Anti-Oriental Immigration Law, which passed the House of Representatives on February 18. The president signed the bill on March 14.

April 26. The Mutual Cooperation Federation published its newspaper, The Kongnip Sinbo, or the Mutual Cooperation News, and the Korean community accepted it well. The office of the federation was moved to San Francisco from Oakland.

May 10. Mr. Song Sok-jun, chairman of the Mutual Cooperation Federation, died.

July 20. Silchi-hoi, or the Practical Society, was organized under the leadership of Pak Sung-nyol at Hilo, on the Island of Hawaii. The purpose of the organization was to encourage Koreans to be practical in order to advance the struggle for Korea's independence.

August 1. Mr. Yi Sang-sol and Mr. Yi Yi-jong, both Korean envoys to the Hague Peace Conference, arrived in New York.

September 2. The representatives of twenty-four Korean organizations met in Honolulu and agreed on a resolution that was the basis for the formation of the Hapsong Hyop-hoi, or the United Federation. This was the first united organization of all Korean organizations that had existed in the Hawaiian Islands. Soon after the establishment of the federation, forty-seven branch offices were organized in various parts of the Hawaiian Islands and the total membership reached 1,051, who paid $2.25 per person per annum.

October. Many Koreans were financially affected by the depression.

October 3. The New Korean World was published by the Great Unity Fatherland Protection Association with its editor, Choi Yong-man and its executive, Mr. Mun Yang-mok. The publication continued until October 23, 1909. On May 10, 1910, it was incorporated into the New Korea.

October 22. The United Federation, Hapsong Hyop-hoi, published its newspaper, the United Korean News, and its editor was Kim Song-kwon. It published sixty issues from October 22, 1907 to January 25, 1909. The newspaper was incorporated into The Sinhan Kukbo, or the United Korean Weekly, on February 15, 1909.

November 17. A group of ten Koreans who went to work in Alaska returned to San Francisco.

1908

January 26. The third annual meeting of the Great Unity Fatherland Protection Association was held in San Francisco. Mr. Paik Il-kyu was elected president and chief editor of the Great Unity Information. Several branch offices were established in Sacramento, Fresno, and Salt Lake City.

An American employed by the Japanese foreign office, Durham W. Stevens, arrived in San Francisco on his way to Washington and had an interview with the correspondent of the San Francisco Chronicle. The newspaper subsequently published his interview. In the interview, Stevens pointed out that the Japanese control of Korea was working for the good of Koreans. The Korean community was outraged by his statement and sent its representatives, Mun Yang-mok, Choi Jong-ik, Chong Ja-kwan, and Yi Hak-hyon, to meet Stevens and demand his apology. As Stevens refused to withdraw his statement, Chong Ja-kwan, one of the representatives, threw blows against Stevens.

March 23. Chang In-whan shot Stevens as he was getting ready to leave San Francisco. Stevens was taken to a nearby hospital for emergency treatment, but he died on March 25 from the wounds he had received. Chang received a sentence of twenty-five years of imprisonment, but later was released on bail on January 14, 1919 and finally released April 11, 1924.

April 8. A group of Korean workers, under the initiative of Kim Kil-yon and Paik Nak-byom, left San Francisco for Alaska

April 9. The New Korean World published its twnety-fifth

issue as its final issue. Financial difficulty prevented further publication.

May 23. The Korean Women's Association was established in San Francisco by Mrs. Yi Min-sik, Mrs. Sin Yun-ho, Mrs. Mun Kyong-ho, Mrs. Chang Hong-bom, and Mrs. Pak Ch'ang-un. The purpose of the organization was to promote Korean language education and to assist in church affairs. Also, the members were determined not to get involved in politics.

June 24. Syngman Rhee received his M.A. degree from Harvard University.

July 13. The Patriotic People's Representative meeting was called by Pak Yong-man.

September. The Prosperity Federation in Honolulu began to publish its newspaper.

September 14. The Korean laborers who had gone to Alaska returned to San Francisco, and the Korean community held a party welcoming their return on September 19.

December 21. The Korean Methodist church in San Francisco began to publish its Great Way, a monthly under the editorship of Yang Ju-sam, for a period of three years.

1909   January 17. The Mutual Cooperation Federation of San Francisco held its representatives' meeting and elected its president and vice president.

February 1. The Mutual Cooperation Federation and the United Federation were merged into one organization. The new organization was called the Korean National Association. The new association elected Chong Myong-won as president of the Hawaii branch and changed the name of the Hanin Hapsong Sinbo, or the United Korean News, to the United Korean Weekly. Its editor was Hong Jong-p'yo. Chong Nae-kwan was elected president of the North American branch and the Kongnip Sinbo, or the Korean News, was changed to the New Korea. Its editor was Choi Jong-ik.

May 5. The Eastern Business Incorporation was organized at the headquarters building of the Korean National Association. The company decided to collect $25,000 as its capital and set the price of a share at $25.00.

June. Pak Yong-man, Pak Ch'o-hu, Im Dong-sik, and
Chong Han-kyong established the Korean Youth Corps with
the permission of the State of Nebraska, and trained Korean
youths in military tactics.

December. Yang Ju-sam, the minister of the San Francisco
Korean Methodist Church, resigned in order to continue his
study in theology and the Reverend Yun Byong-gu succeeded
him.

December. Ahn Sok-jung and Yi Wong-gil, both residents
of Redlands, published their proposal for construction of a
building for the New Korea. The proposal called for a contribution of 30 dollars from 500 people.

December 18. The Korean National Association held its representatives' meeting and elected Whang Sa-yong president
of the North American branch. The Hawaiian branch of the
Korean National Association elected Yi Nae-soo as its president.

1910   January 30. Yun Ch'i-ho, the representative of the Korean
Young Men's Christian Association, arrived in San Francis-
co, by way of Honolulu, to attend the Congress of the World
Sunday School to be held in Washington on May 19.

January 31. A local coal mine in Colorado exploded and
killed approximately 100 miners. Among them were nine
Koreans.

February. Under the initiative of Choi Yong-man, the Han-
Mi Muyok Hoisa, or the Korean-American Trade Company,
was established. The total capital was set at $20,000 and
the price of each share was to be set at $10.00. Choi sold
250 shares and later went back to Korea for business. He
was unable to return as he was refused reentry to the United
States.

February 9. Under the initiative of Ahn Sok-jung, a group
of Korean residents in Redlands area established the Hungop
Jusik Hoisa, or Business Promotion Incorporated. The total
capital was set at $3,000 and each share was to be sold at
a price of $50.00

February 10. Syngman Rhee's book, The Spirit of Independence, was published by the Great Unity New Bookstore in
Los Angeles.

February 10. The Great Unity Fatherland Protection Association was merged with the Korean National Association.

March 1. The T'aedong Sirop Jusik Hoisa, or the Great Eastern Industrial Company, was established to create a military base for the Independence Army, to be under the direction of the Korean National Association. The total capital was set at $50,000 and the price of each share was to be $50.00

March 5. The editor of the United Korean Weekly of Honolulu resigned, and No Jae-ho succeeded Hong Jong-p'yo.

March 21. Yi Hang-wu of London, England arrived in New York and came to San Francisco on April 2. Beginning on May 4, he edited the New Korea with a new English section. But financial difficulty arose and Mr. Choe Jung-ik took it over again.

March 25. Mr. Oh Un, with help from other Koreans, established the Business Encouragement League in Los Angeles and was engaged in agriculture and business. The league was disbanded after five years, as they failed in business.

July 12. Mr. Choi Yong-man left San Francisco for Korea aboard the Manchuria in order to import Korean manufacture. Mr. Choi was an executive of the San Francisco Korean American Trade Company.

The New Korea discontinued its publication between August 10 and September 21 due to financial difficulaties.

Mr. Ahn Sok-jung, a resident of Redlands who had proposed the construction of the New Korea Building, came to visit the Korean community in San Francisco. After he had learned that the newspaper was confronted with financial difficulty, he volunteered to work for a collection of contributions from Koreans toward the newspaper. He later published his report on September 15. His second report was issued on November 16.

July. Korea was annexed by the Japanese Empire. The Mutual Unity Association was convened in Honolulu and later sent letters of protest to the king of Korea, the emperor of Japan, and heads of many governments in Europe and America.

Syngman Rhee received his Ph.D. degree from Princeton
University during the summer and left New York on September 3, arriving in Korea on October 10.

September 19. Whang Sa-yong, president of the Korean National Association of North America, arrived in Honolulu
and visited Korean communities in the islands. He returned
to the Mainland on June 23, 1911.

The Redlands area Korean community was successful in
collecting 30 dollars from 500 supporters to secure a building for the Korean National Association, which also would
serve as the headquarters of the New Korea. A building in
San Francisco was purchased at a price of $3,500, and a
ceremony marking the establishment of the hall was held on
October 1.

November 28. Sarah Choi arrived in Hawaii as a picture
bride. She was the first of the 951 picture brides who came
to Hawaii from Korea. She married Yi Nae-soo.

December 22. The Korean National Association of North
America held its representatives' meeting and elected Mun
Yang-mok as its president. The Hawaiian branch of the association held its meeting and elected Chong Ch'il-nae as
its president.

1911

January. The Hawaii branch of the Korean National Association began to collect contributions that were to be used in
bringing to America Koreans who had emigrated to Mexico.

The Korean minister of Russia, Mr. Yi Bom-jin, committed
suicide protesting against the Japanese annexation of Korea.
His property was sold, and a sum of $3,000 was sent to the
Korean National Association according to his will.

The Reverend Yun Byong-gu resigned from his ministerial
post at the Korean Methodist Church of San Francisco and
the Reverend Yi Dae-wi was chosen as pastor.

March 4. The Korean National Association of Hawaii organized the Hanin Nongsang Jusik Hoisa, or the Korean Agricultural and Commerical Corporation, in order to promote
agriculture and industry. The total capital was set at
$100,000, and the price of each share was set at $10.00.

March. Pak Yong-man, who had established the Korean
Youth Corps at Hastings, Nebraska, took over the editorship of the New Korea.

The Reverend Min Ch'an-ho went to the University of Southern California for study and the Reverence Hong Ch'i-bom
took over the ministerial responsibility at the Korean Christian Church of Honolulu.

March 15. Yi Hang-wu, who had edited the New Korea, went
to Honolulu to edit the United Korean Weekly.

Pak Yong-man, who had edited the New Korea, left and Kang
Bun took over the editorship in July.

The New Korean Company, a branch organization of the
Korean National Association, reported that five hundred
acres of potato fields were cultivated under the auspices of
the company.

September 3. Ahn Ch'ang-ho arrived in New York and came
to San Francisco. He had gone to Korea in January 1907.

Mun Yang-mok, president of the Korean National Association of North America, resigned for personal reasons and
the secretary-general, Kang Bun, took over as acting president.

October. Ho Seung-won and Yi Sun-gi established a department store in Stockton, California and began to provide agricultural supplies to nearby farms.

October 14. A center training Korean students was established in Claremont, California, and a ceremony was held
to mark the opening of the center.

October 31. Kang Bun resigned from his editorial position,
and Hong Jong-p'yo arrived in San Francisco from Honolulu
to edit the New Korea on November 8.

November 22. The Korean National Association held its
delegates' conference in Riverside, and decided to move
the San Francisco Korean National Association to Los Angeles. They also elected Kang Myong-wha as president of
the branch. The Honolulu branch elected Chong Ch'il-nae
as its president.

1912

January 29. According to a news report, Ahn Ch'ang-ho, Kim In-soo, and others organized in Los Angeles the North American Business, Inc. and built up capital for investment in agriculture and business. During World War I the company engaged in rice farming and made a profit. Due to a business failure after the war, the company was reorganized on April 21, 1929.

March 18. Due to financial difficulaties, the United Korean Weekly discontinued its operation. On June 17, the Weekly was republished with Chong Won-do as its editor.

September 16. The Korean Youth Corps, established under the leadership of Pak Yong-man in Hastings, Nebraska, graduated its first class of thirteen students.

November 30. Pak Yong-man became the editor of the United Korean Weekly and went to Honolulu.

December 9. The New Korea was discontinued for a period of six months.

December 13. The North American branch of the Korean National Association held its delegates' conference and elected Chong Won-do as its president, and the Hawaiian branch elected Pak Sang-ha as its president.

1913

April 19. The Korean Women's Association was organized in Honolulu. This was the first Korean women's organization in the Hawaiian Islands. The chairman of the organization was Maria Whang. The purpose of the organization was to promote Korean language education, to refuse things made by Japanese, to assist other social organizations, and to help Koreans who were in need. The organization existed until Marhc 1919, when it was disbanded to join the Korean Ladies Relief Society.

May 13. Hungsa-dan (Corps for the Advancement of Individuals) was organized at the headquarters building of the Korean National Association of North America. The purpose of the organization was to educate people. The chairman of the corps was Hong On, and the chairman of the board of directors was Ahn Ch'ang-ho.

May 19. The Alien Land Act went into effect in California, and Koreans were affected by this law.

June 4. Pak Yong-man organized the first Korean Students Association in North America. The headquarters of the association was located at Hastings, Nebraska, and its president was Pak Ch'o-wu.

June 23. Yi Dae-wi assumed the editorship of the New Korea and began to republish it.

August 1. The Kungmin-bo, or the Korean National Herald, succeeded the United Korean Weekly. Because of the diminishing number of readers willing to support a Korean language newspaper, the publication of this important newspaper was discontinued in December 1968.

A group of eleven Korean workers recruited to work on a farm in the vicinity of Riverside was picketed by a group of local white anti-Oriental citizens. The Korean workers refused to ask the Japanese Consul of Los Angeles, who wanted to represent the Koreans in Los Angeles, to intervene. The Japanese minister to Washington protested against the treatment accorded to Korean workers. But Yi Dae-wi, president of the Korean National Association in San Francisco, sent a cable to William Jennings Bryan, secretary of state, informing him that the Koreans did not want to be represented by the Japanese minister since they were Japanese nationals.

Local Koreans in Danube, California held a week of revival meetings. The Reverend Min Ch'an-ho was invited to the meeting.

The Korean Boarding School, previously established by the Honolulu Korean Methodist Church, was changed to the Central Institute and Syngman Rhee became its principal.

September 20. Syngman Rhee published the Korean Pacific Magazine as a commercial venture. The publication continued for seventeen years, though there were many interruptions. This magazine was followed by the Korean Pacific Weekly, which began publication on December 13, 1930.

Syngman Rhee established the Korean Girls' Seminary in Honolulu. The seminary was then located on the corner of Beretania and Punchbowl Streets. When it opened in the fall of 1913, there were about thirty Korean girls. Dr. Rhee was principal of the seminary. The name of the seminary was later changed to the Korean Christian Institute in September 1918.

1914   April. The Korean National Association sent a sum of
$600 to Koreans suffering from famine in Chientao, China.

June 5. Church services were held at the residence of Mun
Won-ch'il, and the Reverend Whang Sa-yong was invited to
officiate at the church services. On August 10, 1917, the
place of church services was changed to Cho Sung-hak's
residence. The church people appointed Im Jung-gu, a student of the Pacific School of Religion, located in Berkeley,
California, as its pastor.

June 10. The Kungmin Kundan, or the Korean Military
Corps, was organized by Pak Yong-man, who received financial assistance from Pak Chong-soo. The corps was established at Ahemanu near Koolau district on the Island of Oahu,
where Pak Chong-soo operated a Korean camp by contracting for the pineapple fields.

June 25. According to a press release, the building that
housed the Korean National Association headquarters, which
had been purchased in September 1910, was sold at a price
of $3,692. The headquarters then was moved to a building
located on Market and Sixth Streets.

July 23. Paik Il-kyu assumed the responsibility of editing
the New Korea.

August 30. Five hundred Koreans in Hawaii were present
at the opening ceremony of the Korean Military Corps, and
180 students participated in the parade.

September 3. The Korean Students' Friendship Association
was organized by students of the Korean Central Institute
of Honolulu.

October 5. The Korean Students' Friendship Association
published a student bulletin written in Korean.

October 24. The Central Institute, under the directorship
of Syngman Rhee, built a new girls dormitory and held a
ceremony to dedicate the new building.

December. Under the initiative of Ahn Chae-ch'ang, Im

Jong-soon, Choi Kyong-o, and Yi Myong-sop, the Hanin
Nongop Jusik Hoisa, or the Korean Agricultural Corporation,
was organized. The total capital was set at $10,000 and
the price of each share was set at $10.00. They collected
the anticipated capital and began to cultivate vegetables in
Nebraska.

December 9. A new building to house the Korean National
Association headquarters was finished with the funds contributed by Koreans in Hawaii, and a ceremony dedicating
the building was held.

December 22. According to a press release, Yi Dae-wi
was elected president of the Korean National Association
of North America for the following year, and Kim Jong-hak
was elected president of the Korean National Association
in Hawaii for the same year.

A new building was purchased by the Korean National Association in San Francisco at a price of $6,500, and the build-
ing was to be used for housing the headquarters of the Korean National Association as well as the San Francisco Korean Church.

1915   January 7. Paik Il-kyu resigned from the Editorship of the
        New Korea and entered the University of California.

        Early February. The Korean Business Encouragement
        League in Los Angeles purchased two hundred acres of
        land in Louisiana.

        Yi Dae-wi, president of the Korean National Association
        of North America, studied the method of printing newspaper
        in the Han'gul using an Intertype machine, and the New Ko-
        rea was printed by this machine beginning March 11.

        April 21. Choi Jong-ik returned to San Francisco from a
        business trip that took him to Tahiti in the South Pacific.

        April 22. Ahn Ch'ang-ho and Pak Yong-man were elected
        chairman and vice-chairman, respectively, of the central
        headquarters of the Korean National Association, according
        to a report released.

        June 11. Pak Yong-man, editor of the Korean National
        Herald in Honolulu, arrived in San Francisco in order to

attend the ceremony inaugurating members of the central
committee of the Korean National Association.

July 12. Mr. Oh Jin-guk, a resident of Stockton, arrived
in San Francisco and met Mr. Pak Yong-man at a local
hotel, and maligned Mr. Pak. He left for Honolulu on September 28 aboard the Sonoma, but before he reached his
destination, he committed suicide by jumping overboard.
It was alleged that he was on his way to Honolulu to kill
Syngman Rhee.

Ahn Ch'ang-ho visited Honolulu in order to straighten out
the conflict at the Korean National Association of Hawaii
involving misappropriation of funds. Ahn returned on December 21.

1916   January 2. According to a press release, Mr. Kang So-
yong was elected chairman of the Korean National Association of North America, while Mr. Hong Han-sik was elected
chairman of the Korean National Association of Hawaii.

Mr. Song Hon-joo, a student of Roanoke College, was invited to become the minister for the Korean Christian
church of Honolulu.

February 22. According to a press release, a group of
sixty Koreans residing in Manteca, California, rented a total of 1,300 acres of land in order to grow sugar beets.
Sin Kyong-whan, Ha Yong-suk, Kim Su-man and Yi Sung-
no rented a total of 320 acres of land.

February 29. Mr. Choi Jong-ik, who had visited Tahiti for
business purposes, left San Francisco for Honolulu with
Mr. Suh P'il-soon, who was a ginseng merchant. They were
joined by Han Jae-myong at Honolulu and the group left for
Australia. Mr. Han returned in September of the following
year to Honolulu; Mr. Suh went to Singapore, while Mr.
Choi returned to Korea.

March 10. Two Korean ladies arrived in San Francisco
from Shanghai and on March 11, two Korean ladies and
eleven Korean students arrived in San Francisco from Shanghai aboard the China.

May 16. Five Korean ladies and twenty-three Korean students arrived in San Francisco from Shanghai.

May 18. According to a press release, a group of Koreans planned to cultivate 292 acres of land in Nevada for the purpose of growing melons. Among those who planned to cultivate them were Im Jun-gi, Kim In-soo, Pak Yong-sun and Hyon Seung-yol. They had one hundred acres of land.

July 13. The Korean Students' Baseball Club was organized by students in Honolulu.

September. A social club was organized by Cho Sung-whan in Los Angeles and continuted to operate until 1918.

September 28. According to a press release, a group of Koreans planned to cultivate a total of 1,400 acres of land for the purpose of growing rice. Mr. Yi Sun-ki cultivated 640 acres of land in Woodland, California, while Yim Sun-bong and Um Dae-song cultivated 110 acres at Colusa, California. Others cultivated for the purpose of growing beans. Pak Seung-ch'ol and Kim Du-ok cultivated 80 acres of land in the vicinity of Live Oak, California.

September 30. A group of sixteen men and ten women and children arrived in San Francisco aboard the China, but three were repatriated.

October 27. The Korean Students' Friendship Association was organized in San Francisco.

December 5. Noh Baek-nin, Cho Yong-ha and Cho Myong-guk arrived in Honolulu from Shanghai aboard the China.

1917   January 20. The Puk-Mi Sirop Jusik Hoisa, or the North American Industrial Corporation, was organized by Ahn Ch'ang-ho, Song Jong-ik, Maeng Jong-ho, Kim In-soo, Chong Bong-kyu, and others who were members of the Hung-sa-dan. The total capital was set at $95,000 and the price of each share was set at $100.00. The stocks were sold in two separate periods. A total of 4,500 stocks were sold during the first period and the rest of the stocks were sold during the second period. The capital was invested in the cultivation of rice. In 1920, the company took a loss in the rice business and went out of business eventually. Approximately 15¢ was allotted to each share when the company went out of business.
Yi Dae-wi was elected chairman of the All-Korean National Association of North American and Ahn Jung-hyon was elec-

ted chairman of the All-Korean National Association of Hawaii.

March 8. According to a press release, Koreans in Stockton and Manteca areas in California cultivated a total of 3,920 acres of land for sugar beets.

March 29. A group of Korean women in Sacramento established the Korean Women's Association and the chairman of the organization was Yang Che-hyon. The purpose of the organization was to assist the Korean National Association and to refuse to buy things made by the Japanese.

April 26. According to a press release, rice cultivation by Koreans in the state of California was expanding rapidly. Thus Kim Chong-nim, who had made a big profit from rice cultivation, decided to expand his acreage to 2,815 acres.

July 19. A Korean came to San Francisco from Shanghai on the Equator, and on July 20, the China brought from Shanghai to San Francisco, a group of fourteen Korean men, three women, and four girls to be married.

August 28. Cho Sung-whan, a resident of Los Angeles, was invited to join the Central Institute as a Chinese character teacher and left for Honolulu. He returned to Los Angeles on September 4th of the following year.

Ahn Ch'ang-ho, chairman of the Central Headquarters of the Korean National Association, left for Mexico on the San Jose and visited Korean residents in Mexico, and returned to San Francisco on August 29 of the following year.

October 1. A group of seventeen Korean men, two women, eight girls to be married, and four children arrived in San Francisco from Shanghai aboard the China.

October 29. The All-Korean National Association of Hawaii sent Pak Yong-man as its delegate to the Conference of the League of Small Nations to be held in New York.

1918   May 1. The Korean Students' Friendship Association was organized in Columbus, Ohio.

August 18. The Korean Students' Friendship Association was organized in Danube, California.

September 22. A Korean church in Manteca, California was dedicated.

October 8. The Korean Students Association was organized in Chicago, Illinois.

November 28. The Korean Pacific Times, a weekly, was established by Pak Yong-man and his colleagues. The publication continued until March 15, 1926.

Syngman Rhee, Chong Han-kyong, and Min Ch'an-ho were elected as Korean delegates to attend the Peace Conference in Paris, but they were unable to attend the conference as they were refused passports by the U.S. Government.

Within the Korean Methodist Church of Honolulu, established in 1905, there soon occurred an ideological conflict over the issue of church administration and policy. Syngman Rhee argued that the church should not be interfered with by supervision of Superintendent Fry. Fry, on the other hand, wanted to have a tight control over church administration. The supporters of Syngman Rhee seceded from the church and established Shinlip-kyohoi or the New Church on July 29, 1918. The first annual delegates' conference was held on December 23 and the name of the church was changed to the Korean Christian Church. The church held Korean language classes for children until 1941.

1919   Yi Dae-wi remained chairman of the All-Korean National Association of North America, while Yi Jong-kwan was elected chairman of the All-Korean National Assocation of Hawaii.

Syngman Rhee arrived in San Francisco aboard the Enterprise from Honolulu and held a conference with key members of the Korean National Association. He went to Los Angeles on his way to Washington, D.C.

February 20. A group of Korean students in Ohio decided to publish an English journal, the Young Korea, to report to the world Korean social and political conditions, while the Paris Peace Conference was being held.

March 2. A group of Korean women in Danube, California met together to establish the New Korean Women's Association. The founding members were among others, Kang

Won-sin, Hang Song-son, Kim Hye-won, Han Yong-sook, Han Sin-ae and Kim Kyong-ae. The purpose of the organization was to encourage and promote the spirit of independence and to assist the Korean National Association in its effort to restore Korea's independence.

March 9. Ahn Ch'ang-ho, the chairman of the central headquarters of the Korean National Association, received a telegram sent to him by Hyon Sun dated March 1. The telegram stated that the Korean Independence League declared the independence of Korea at 1:00 P.M. on March 1, under the leadership of Son Byong-hi, Yi Sang-je and Gil Son-ju.

Kim Jong-jin was sent to various parts on the West coast by the central headquarters of the Korean National Association in San Francisco to collect contributions from Koreans for independence funds. During a period of sixty-three days, he visited approximately 327 Koreans and returned to San Francisco on May 23, with almost $10,000.

March 20. The New Korea, a weekly newspaper, changed its schedule of publication to every other day in order to report social and political conditions of Korea to Koreans in America. Yi Sal-um assumed the editorial responsibility.

March 24. Kim Kyu-sik sent a telegram to the Korean National Association asking for his delegate credential. He was dispatched to Paris to attend the Peace Conference as a delegate from the provisional Korean government-in-exile.

March 28. A group of Korean women in Los Angeles organized the Women's Friendship Association, and the chairman of the organization was Im Wha-yon. The purpose of the organization was to promote friendship among Koreans, to support social and church activities, to refuse to buy things made by Japanese, to save money by serving meatless dishes on Tuesday and Friday every week, and to help every member of the famliy save money to be sent for the Korean Independence Movement.

April. The central headquarters of the Korean National Association decided to call upon Chinese in America to make contributions for Korea's independence, and Hong On, Kim Yong-hun, and Kang Yong-gak were elected as members of the Chinese Negotiation Committee.

April 14-16. The First Korean Congress was held in Philadelphia with approximately 150 Koreans gathered to make
an appeal to Americans and their government.

May 1. Ahn Ch'ang-ho left San Francisco and arrived in
Shanghai on May 24, aboard the Manila. In Shanghai, he
worked with the Korean provisional government-in-exile.

May 16. The League of the Firends of Korea was organized
by Dr. Floyd W. Tomkins. One of the objectives of the
league was to inform the American public as to the true conditions in the Far East. Other objectives were to secure
religious liberty for the Korean Christians and to extend
sympathy and encouragement to the oppressed people of Korea in their struggle for freedom.

May 18. The Korean Women's Association of Sacramento
and the New Korean Women's Association of Danube sent to
all other Korean Women's organizations a report urging
them to join their effort to create an organization which
would unite all the organizations.

May 26. According to a report made by the central headquarters of the Korean National Association, a total of
$30,389.25 was collected as contributions to the indepen-
dence fund.

May 27. The central headquarters of the Korean National
Association dispatched Kang Yong-so and Whang Sa-yong
to Honolulu in order to discuss social and political conditions with Koreans in the islands.

The Young Korea, an English monthly published by Korean
students in Ohio, changed its original name and began to
appear as The Korea Review, beginning with its June issue.
The editor of the review was Dr. Philip Jaisohn, and it continued until January 1922.

July 2. Yi Sal-um resigned as editor of The New Korea and
on July 24, Kim Hyon-gu assumed the editorial responsibility.

Sometime in the middle of July, Pak Yong-man, the editor
of The Korean National Herald in Honolulu , left for the
Far East.

August 2. Representatives from various Korean women's organizations gathered together in Danube, California and held a conference to establish the Korean Women's Patriotic League. This was the first organization that united all other Korean women's organizations in North America. The Korean Women's Patriotic League was officially established on August 5.

August 15. The Korean Commission was established in Washington, D.C.

August 22. Kim Kyu-sik, ambassador plenipotentiary, who had been dispatched to the Paris Peace Conference, arrived in New York and went to Washington, D.C.

Choi Jae-hyong, finance minister of the Korean provisional government-in-exile, delegated the business of raising money for independence funds to the Korean National Association.

September 1. Dr. Syngman Rhee, as president of the Republic of Korea, issued bonds to raise money for Korea's independence, and all business details were to be administered by the Korean Commission in Washington, D.C.

September 26. Under the auspices of the Korean Students' Friendship Association of San Francisco, the Korean Students Delegates Conference was held to discuss ways and means to unite various Korean students' organizations. The conference decided to establish a communication committee and elected its members, who were charged with the responsibility of contacting as many Korean students as they could so that they could join the unity movement. Although the All Korean Students Organization Convention was held on April 6, 1920, the convention participants were unable to organize the All-Korean Students Association in America.

October 11. The Korean Friendship Association was organized with the assistance of Henry Chung at the Hotel San Francisco in San Francisco.

Kim Kyu-sik, chairman of the Korean Commission, visited the Korean National Association of San Francisco during his tour around the state of California and urged Koreans to make contributions for the cause of Korea's independence.

October 29. Yi Ui-kong, president of the Korean Red Cross,
arrived in Seattle from Shanghai and made a tour to collect
contributions. According to a report made on December 9,
the total contribution amounted to $10,300.

November 23. According to a news report, the contributions made in Hawaii as of the end of October for Korea's
independence funds amounted to $34,034.05, which was con-
tributed by 2,907 persons.

December 29. According to a report made by the central
headquarters of the Korean National Association, the total
revenue was $88,013,50, and the expenditures were as fol-
lows: $32,600 for the Korean provisional government and
the Korean Commission in Washington, D.C., $14,000 for
diplomacy and publicity, $8,500 for dispatching representa-
tives to the Far East and Europe, $13,500 for travel ex-
penses, $500 for relief, and $2,600 for communication.

The rice cultivation by Koreans in California was successful
this year. As a result, many Koreans contributed toward
Korea's independence funds. A total of $42,955 was col-
lected; the maximum contribution made by a single person
was $3,400, and the average contribution was $350.

1920   January 1. According to a press release, Kang Yong-so
was elected president of the All-Korean National Association of North America, while Yi Jong-kwan was elected president of the All-Korean National Association of Hawaii.

Hong On, who was elected a member of the Chinese Negotiation Committee, made a tour in Oregon, Washington,
Utah, and Idaho in order to encourage Chinese to make contributions for the cause of Korea's independence. He returned from this trip to San Francisco on January 22, and
left for another tour on March 10.

January 26. The president of the Common League of Honolulu, Son Yong-whan, sent a telegram to Yun Byong-gu,
president of the All Korean National Association of San Francisco requesting him to disband the All-Korean National Association of Hawaii. Upon the receipt of such a request,
Yun appointed a special investigation committee, composed
of Whang Sa-yong, Chong Ch'il-nae, Chong Won-myong,
Ahn Won-gyu, Song Yong-whan, Yi Nae-soo, and Yun Kye-
sang, which was charged with the task of investigating the

administration of the All-Korean National Association of
Hawaii as well as of the Common League.

February 20. The School of Aviation was established in
Willows, California under the initiative of Kim Chong-nim
and Noh Baek-nin, who was chief of the Bureau of Military
Affairs of the Korean provisional government-in-exile. Kim
Chong-nim, a rich businessman who made money from rice
cultivation, donated three airplanes and made a monthly contribution of $3,000 for maintenance and operation of the
school.

The Han-Mi Po, or the Korean-American News, a weekly
paper, was published between May 12, 1920 and September
14, 1921. The editor of the paper, Song Yong-whan, used
the paper to criticize Syngman Rhee.

June 22. Syngman Rhee accompanied by Henry Chung, left
San Francisco and arrived in Honolulu on June 29.

July 16. Noh Baek-nin, who had supervised the training of
Korean pilots in Willows, California, arrived in Honolulu.

October 3. Kim Kyu-sik left for the Far East and Hyon Sun,
who had come to America last April, assumed the acting
chairmanship of the Korean Commission.

In the early part of November, Syngman Rhee and No Baek-
nin left Honolulu for Shanghai and arrived there on December 8.

Koreans scattered around Northern California were engaged
in rice cultivation on approximately 7,990 acres. However,
in early November, rain and hail interrupted their rice har-
vest and they were unable to complete it. Korean farmers
never recovered from this great financial loss.

November 12. The Federated Investment Company was organized in Willows, California by Yun Byong-gu, Kim Chong-
nim, Hong Jong-man and Chong Mong-nong. Yun Byong-gu
was elected president of the company.

November 18. The Department of Finance of the Korean
provisional government-in-exile awarded Kim Chong-nim,
Kim Sung-sil, Sin Kwang-hi and Im Jun-gi a letter of thanks
for their contributions. They received the award because

each of them made a contribution of more than one thousand dollars.

Choi Jin-ha was elected president of the All-Korean National Association of North America, according to a report made on November 23.

The Korean Commission made a financial report on revenue and expenditures between December 1919 and November 1920. According to the report, a total of $70,190 was collected by the commission, and expenditures totaled $65,230. The report indicated that Koreans in Hawaii, Mexico, and the continental U.S.A. bought the public bonds issued by Syngman Rhee, which totaled $46,404, and a sum of $15,987 was collected from Chinese residents in America.

According to the census report of the fourteenth census, there were 1,224 Koreans in the continental U.S.A.

Charles Ho Kim and Kim Hyong-soon established Kim Brothers Company in Reedley, California. The company had a nursery and was engaged in fruit packing. As one of the most successful businesses owned by persons of Korean ancestry in America, the annual income was estimated at one million dollars in 1958.

1921   January 6. According to a report made on this day, the construction cost for the Korean Christian Institute was set at $85,000; $35,00 was to be collected from among Koreans, and $50,000 was to be contributed by Americans. The Chamber of Commerce of Honolulu gave $50,000 to the board of trustees of the institute.

January 17. Kim Hyon-gu resigned from The New Korea as its editor, and Kim Nyo-sik assumed the editorial responsibility.

March 21. The All-Korean National Association of Hawaii was changed to the Korean Residents Association. Min Ch'an-ho and Ahn Won-gyu were elected president and vice-president, respectively.

Henry Chung published The Case of Korea, which informed the American public of the Japanese treatment of Koreans. He received an honorary doctorate from the American University for writing this book.

April 30. The Korean Students Association in North America was organized, and Yi Yong-jik and Cho Byong-ok were elected president and vice-president, respectively. The organization took place one year after the initial campaign to unite all Korean students associations had been launched. The headquarters of the association was located in New York City. In 1923, the headquarters was moved to Chicago.

May 10. The Korean Students Association was organized in Honolulu, Hawaii.

Early June. Hong On, a member of the Chinese Negotiation Committee, left New York for Panama, Peru, Chile, and Ecuador to visit Chinese residents there in order to encourage them to make contributions for Korea's independence.

June 29. Syngman Rhee returned to Honolulu from Shanghai.

July 7. The Dongji-hoi, or the Comrade Society, was organized, and it published its rules.

August 18. Syngman Rhee left Honolulu for San Francisco and from there he left for Washington, D.C.

November 21. According to a report made on this day, Kang Yong-sung and Kim Hyon-gu were elected president and vice-president, respectively, of the All-Korean National Association of North America.

Kang Yong-gak was responsible for the publication of a students' bulletin called The Young Korea. The bulletin was published twice a year and it existed for a period of six years.

1922   February. The Nam-Gaju Nongsan Chohap, or the Southern California Agricultural Association, was organized by Song Jong-ik, Yi Du-song, and Song Sang-dae in Los Angeles. The association was engaged in the wholesale fruit business.

March 26. The Korean Methodist Church of Reedley, California was established. Since February 1919, a group of Korean residents in Reedley had met together for the purpose of conducting church services. They met at the residence of Chon Song-yong and later moved their place of service to the Kim Brothers Company. The members of the church contacted the Methodist Mission, which assisted

them in establishing the church. However, due to a dispute
in June 1936, over the issue of emperor worship, the Korean church members seceded from the Methodist Mission.
The members chose to join the Korean Presbyterian Church
of Danube. In October 1938, the Korean population increased
to eleven families, which necessitated the establishment of
a church. Therefore, with financial assistance from the
Kim Brothers, a church building was constructed and the
ceremony dedicating the new building was held on March 1,
1939. This was the beginning of the Korean Presbyterian
Church of Reedley.

The publication of The New Korea was discontinued between
April 10 and August 10.

October 19. A Korean Students Association was organized
in Los Angeles, California.

Choi Jin-ha was elected president of the All-Korean National
Association of North America.

An English publication, the Korean Students' Bulletin, was
published in New York. Its editor was Pak Jin-sop, who
was later replaced by Whang Ch'ang-ha. The publication
continued for a period of five years.

1923   February 10. A group of Korean residents in New York
City bought a building on West 21st Street with financial assistance from the Methodist Mission at a cost of $18,000.
In October 1927, the church was moved to a building located
on West 115th Street purchased at a cost of $45,000.

A home visiting baseball team was organized. It was composed of students attending the Korean Christian Institute in
Honolulu. The team led by Min Ch'an-ho, Nodie Kim, and
Kim Yong-wu left for Korea on June 20 in order to raise
money for the construction of a building to house the Korean
Christian Institute. The team had exhibition baseball games
in Korea. During its tour, it collected a total of $25,770.13
and used $9,613 as its travel expenses. The rest was used
for construction.

August. The Dongyang Singmul Jusik Hoisa, or the Oriental
Food Products Corporation, was established in Chicago by
Chong T'ae-un, Oh Han-soo, Kim Hong-ki, Cho Jong-jin,
and Whang Whue. The total capital was set at $15,000 and

the price of each share was set at $50. The capital was in-
vested in the business of producing chop suey and other
Oriental food.

November 22. The president of the League of Friends of
Korea, Dr. Tomkins, sent his protest to Secretary of State
Hughes, charging the Japanese with the crime of killing in-
nocent Koreans during the Tokyo earthquake.

1924   March 8. There was an explosion in the Castle Gate Mine
in Utah, and approximately 170 miners were killed by the
explosion. Three Korean miners, Yi Yong-sun, Um Jung-
ch'il, and Yu Gong-wu, were among them.

The Korean National Association received a total of
$1,346.25 from the Dong-A Ilbo, which had organized a
campaign to collect money to help Koreans abroad. The
Korean National Association distributed the money to various Korean language schools and a sum of $2,500 was
sent to the Korea Christian Institute in Honolulu.

May 15. The Oriental Exclusion Law was passed and immigration of Koreans and of picture brides came to an end.

July 5. So Hak-bin, one-time resident of America, arrived
in Seattle with his wife, whom he had married during his
visit home. He and his wife were refused reentry due to
the new immigration law that went into effect on July 1.

December 16. Ahn Ch'ang-ho, who had left for Shanghai
on May 1, 1919, returned to San Francisco.

July 27. A Korean Methodist church was formed in Chicago,
under the initiative of Kang Yong-so, Kim Kyong, Pak
Jang-soon, Ch'a Ui-sok, Kim Won-yong, Cho Hi-nyom,
and Yom Kwang-sop. The church held its services in the
basement of an American church building located at Lincoln
Avenue. The Reverend Kim Ch'ang-jun officiated at the
church services.

A Korean baseball team composed of thirteen players arrived in Honolulu and played exhibition games. The team
left Honolulu on July 28.

November 23. Syngman Rhee made a report to a conference of the Dongji-hoi in order to expand the society's ac-

tivities. Out of this meeting emerged the organization of the Dongji Siksan Hoisa, or the Comrades Society's Investment Corporation, in March 1925. The corporation was duly organized by selling 100 shares for $100 per share, and it was incorporated for twenty-five years under the laws of the Territory of Hawaii on February 4, 1926. The capital stock was limited to $70,000. The corporation bought 930 acres of land at Olaa, Hawaii, eighteen miles from Hilo, and there established an ideal farm village called the Dongji Ch'on, or the Comrades Society's Village. The corporation went out of business in 1931.

1925   Koreans in Los Angeles sent a sum of $1,421 to the Relief Association Headquarters in Seoul to help Koreans in their fight against famine.

July 1. Dr. Philip Jaisohn attended the Pan-Pacific Conference held in Honolulu.

Pak Yong-man, who had gone to the Far East on July 8, 1919, came back to Honolulu and left for the Far East again in March of 1926.

The Korean National Association collected a total of $700 and sent it to the Dong-A Ilbo in order to help Koreans who suffered financial loss from flood.

Paĭk Il-Kyu was elected president of the All-Korean National Association of North America for 1926, and he remained in that post until 1934.

1926   Peter Hyon established the Dongyang Singmul Jusik Hoisa, or the Oriental Food Products Corporation, in Los Angeles. The corporation is still engaged in growing beansprouts, and mushrooms, and producing chop suey and chow mein. The total assets were estimated at two million dollars as of 1958.

February 20. Ahn Ch'ang-ho, who had returned from the Far East on December 16, left for the Far East again.

Early June. According to a report released at this time, seven persons of Korean ancestry were in the employ of the Hawaiian Department of Public Instruction.

Although the Korean provisional government-in-exlie had

issued an order disbanding the Korean Mission in Washington, D.C., the commission continued its activities and a member of the commission, Kim Hyon-gu, bought a building to house the commission for $18,500.

1927   January 16. The secretary-general of the Yuhan Company located in Detroit, left San Francisco for Korea. The purpose of his trip was to study the potential import of raw materials from Korea.

March 9. The name of the Korean Students' Association was changed to the Great Korean Students' Association of North America. A total of 255 students were registered as its members.

June 27. Choi Rin, one of the thirty-three representatives who signed their names on the Declaration of Independence on March 1, 1919, arrived in San Francisco. He came to visit Koreans on his around-the-world trip.

July 1. A club called the Rose of Sharon Club was organized in Honolulu, Hawaii.

Dr. Han Yong-dae, a graduate of Stanford University Medical School, had completed his internship at a hospital in Peking and returned to Los Angeles. Upon his return, he passed the California state medical examination, and established his own practice.

1928   January 18. A group of Koreans in Stockton, California organized the Mutual Relief Society and began to save money for the purpose of helping each other.

According to a report in early March, the Chung-an Company had expanded its business with $300,000 capital. The company began its wholesale business of producing chop suey in 1922. Chong Yang-p'il, Ahn Jae-ch'ang, and Cho Oh-hung were three people who went into business together.

June 29. The Samil Sinbo, the Samil News, was issued in New York by a group of Koreans. Among them were Chang Dok-su, Yun Ch'i-yong, Ho Jung, Hong Duk-su, Yi Bong-su, and Kim Yang-su. Ho Jung later served the Republic of Korea in various official positions including that of prime minister.

July 17. Kim Hong-bom, a Korean resident in Peking, sent a cablegram to the headquarters of the Independence League of Hawaii, and informed them that Pak Yong-man had been assassinated.

November 28. Dr. Kim Yong-sun, a graduate of the Harvard University Medical School, passed the California state medical examination and began his own practice.

December 24. The Mutual Relief Society held its second regular meeting at the Korean church building in Stockton. A total of twenty-three persons attended the meeting. It was reported to the meeting that a total of $3,940 was in its savings account.

1930   According to a report made on January 1, the Mutual Relief Society, established in January 1928, had grown rapidly and had a total of $4,300 in its savings account.

June 9. Sin Hung-wu, who had worked as secretary of the Korean YMCA for the past ten years, received an honorary doctorate from his alma mater, the University of South Carolina.

Koreans in Northern California were again successful in their rice cultivation. Han Sung-jun cultivated 600 acres in the Dunnigan area, Kang Dae-gun farmed 300 acres in C Colusa, Pak Ul-sok cultivated 400 acres in the Maxwell area, Yi Jae-soo cultivated 700 acres in the Arbuckle area and Chong Mong-nong cultivated 600 acres in the Merced area.

Younghill Kang published The Grass Roof, which was well accepted by the American public.

According to the fifteenth census report, there were 1,860 Koreans in the continental U.S.A.

October 16. A Korean Methodist church was established in Los Angeles. The members of this newly established church were originally members of the Korean Presbyterian Church of Los Angeles. However, due to an ideological conflict on the question of support for Syngman Rhee, the membership was divided into two groups: one supporting Syngman Rhee, and the other opposing him. On October 14, 1924, the group supporting Syngman Rhee occupied the church building of the Korean Presbyterian Church by force and drove out the members of the group opposing Syngman Rhee. The ousted group established a church immediately after the incident, and they later changed the name of the church to the Free Church. This Free Church later became the Korean Methodist Church of Los Angeles.

1931   March 1. Koreans on the Island of Kauai organized Dan Hap-hoi, or the United Society, on the occasion of the twelfth anniversary of the Korean Declaration of Independence on March 1, 1919. Yi Hong-ki was elected president of the society.

According to a report made on April 23, a building in Chicago was bought for $18,000 to be used as the Korean church building.

September 18. The Manchurian Incident was triggered by the Japanese occupation of Mukden, and Koreans abroad resolved to cooperate with the Chinese to defeat the common enemy.

Syngman Rhee left Honolulu for the easter region of the United States to launch his campaign against Japanes encroachment in Manchuria.

December 20. The Mutual Relief Society in Stockton held its annual meeting. One of the critical issues in the meeting was a discussion on whether or not the society should continue under the present difficult financial conditions. The issue was settled by a majority vote which decided to maintain the society.

1932   In 1931, Kim Koo, then minister of home affairs and minister of war of the Korean provisional government-in-exile in Shanghai, had asked the Dan Hap-hoi of Kauai for a large sum of money to support his contemplated trip to Moscow to see Stalin. The United Society of Kauai raised one thousand dollars and sent it to Mr. Kim Koo who spent it in planning and executing assassinations of Japanese military leaders. On January 1, 1932, Yi Bong-ch'ang, a member of the "suicide squad" of the Korean provisional government army, threw a bomb into the midst of an imperial procession and killed General Sirakawa, the Japanese commander-in-chief and General Kawahara. The bomb was manufactured with the funds Kim Koo received from the United Society of Kauai.

December 23. Syngman Rhee left New York for Geneva.

Tai Sung Lee, executive secretary for the Korean Student Christian Movement of Hawaii, began to publish the Korean Students of Hawaii Yearbook.

1933   January 16. The name of the Korean Residents Association, which came into being on March 22, 1922, was changed to its original name, Kungmin-hoi, or the Korean National Association, by the decision made by the Congress of the Korean Resiadents Association.

January 19. The Second Congress of the Dongji-hoi was held in Honolulu and discussions on foreign policy, development of the society, and revision of the society's constitution took place.

December 24. The University of Chicago held a conference of Oriental students. Students from eleven different countries attended. Mary Kim of the University of Michigan attended the conference and played a traditional Korean instrument.

1934   January 6. The Board of Trustees of the Mutual Relief Society in Stockton held its board meeting in order to take care of the society's annual business. The revenue of the society was $2,731 and expenditures were $804. The society had a total of $1,926 in its savings account.

April 26. Yi Jong-gon, president of the All-Korean National Association of Hawaii, and his staff members resigned from their official positions due to lack of financial support for the organization. Their resignation was accepted by the headquarters of the All-Korean National Association. An election was held on June 15 to elect a president of the organization. Kim Yun-bae was elected president of the All-Korean National Association of Hawaii.

August 4. The Congress of Women of the Pan-Pacific was held in Honolulu, and Bernice Kim, Sally Kim, both from Hawaii, and Mary Kim, of the University of Michigan, attended the meeting as representatives from Korea.

August 7. Agnes Davies, a young American woman determined to marry a Korean whom she had met at Drew University in Madison, New Jersey, where both were students,

arrived in Korea in order to fulfill her marriage vow. Later, she wrote a book, I Married a Korean, which was published in 1953 by the John Day Company.

October 8. Syngman Rhee married an Austrian woman by
the name of Francesca Donner. This marriage drew a
great deal of criticism from Korean residents in Hawaii and
the continental U.S.A. Previously, Rhee denounced inter-
marriage and encouraged young Koreans to maintain their
racial purity.

1935   January 5. The Delegates Conference of the Korean National
Association was held in San Francisco. During the conference Choi Jin-ha was elected president to succeed the out-
going president, Paĭk Il-gyu.

November 28. The thirtieth anniversary of the beginning of
Korean immigration was held in the Korean Methodist Church
of Los Angeles.

1936   Ahn Ik-t'ae, a Korean resident in Philadelphia, completed
his composition of the Korean national anthem, according
to a press release on March 26.

July 4. A special delegates' conference of the Korean National Association was held in San Francisco. The special
conference dealt with nine major agenda items. Among
them were revision of the constitution of the association,
problems of educating the second-generation Koreans, social services for the aged, financial support for the Korean
provisional government-in-exile, adoption of the committee
system, and construction of a building to house the headquarters of the Korean National Association.

September. A Korean Christian church was established in
Los Angeles. Later in 1943, there occurred an ideological
struggle on the issue of support for Syngman Rhee. The
members of Dongji-hoi, an organization created by Syngman
Rhee for his political activities, pulled their membership
out of this church and established another church with an
identical name.

1937   Bernice B. H. Kim completed her unpublished study, The
Koreans in Hawaii, submitted to the University of Hawaii
in partial requirement for the degree of master of arts.

January 3. The First Delegates Conference of the Korean
National Association was held in San Francisco according
to the revised constitution, and an election was held to
choose a chairman of the Central Executive Committee and
a secretary of the Standing Department. Kim Ho was elected
chairman of the Central Executive Committee, and Choi Jin-
ha was elected secretary of the Standing Deparmtnet.

All business relating to the Mutual Relief Society of Stockton
was turned over to the Korean National Association for the
purpose of expanding social service for the aged and others
in need.

October 21. Haan Kil-soo, a Korean resident in Hawaii,
made a charge during his testimony before the Congressional
Statehood Committee that the Japanese government, through
its Honolulu consulate, attempted to unite Orientals in Hawaii against the whites. The charge was immediately denied by Tsueneshiro Yamazaki, vice-consul of the Japanese
Consulate in Honolulu, who termed it ridiculous.

December 22. The All-Korean National Association of San
Francisco moved to a new building located on Jefferson Boulevard in Los Angeles.

1938   April 17. A ceremony dedicating a new building to house
the headquarters of the All-Korean National Association
was held in Los Angeles.

April 24. A church ceremony dedicating a new church
building of the Korean Christian church constructed at a
cost of $40,821.73 was held in Honolulu, Hawaii. The
church building was constructed on Liliha Street, and the
cornerstone of the building was laid on October 3, 1937.
The seating capacity of the building was from 600 to 800.

May 1. A ceremony dedicating the Korean Presbyterian
Church of Los Angeles was held with the Reverend Kim
Sung-nak officiating.

November 20. Younghill Kang, the author of The Grass
Roof, spoke at the headquarters of the All-Korean National
Association of Los Angeles. He made a statement to the
effect that whoever wants to go into the field of English literature should cultivate his self-confidence.

1939   January 1. The Delegates Conference of the Korean National
            Association was held to discuss the association's business
            and elected Song Hon-joo as chairman of the Central Execu-
            tive Committee.

            March 1. A ceremony dedicating a new Korean Presbyterian
            church building was held in Reedley, which became the cen-
            ter of Korean residents in central California. The Kim bro-
            thers who had a business in Reedley helped to build this Ko-
            rean community.

            December 31. The Delegates Conference of the Korean Na-
            tional Association was held in order to discuss budgetary
            problems. The following year's budget was passed and Han
            Si't'ae was elected chairman of the Central Executive Com-
            mittee.

1940   According to a press release on February 1, a group of Ko-
            rean residents in Los Angeles organized a society to help
            victims of drought in Korea. It collected money as well as
            relief goods both from Koreans and Americans with the as-
            sistance of the Golden Rule Foundations in New York.

            September 7. Haan Kil-soo urged Koreans in Hawaii regis-
            tering as aliens under the Alien Registration Act of 1940 to
            register as Koreans and not as Japanese subjects. Subse-
            quently, Earl G. Harrison, director of Alien Registration
            in Washington, D.C., ruled that Koreans have the right to
            register as Koreans and not as Japanese subjects.

1941   Haan Kil-soo charged that Japan had been making prepara-
            tions to attack the United States and that between 35,000 and
            50,000 Japanese in the Hawaiian Islands who either were ci-
            tizens of Japan or held dual citizenship were prepared to as-
            sist Japan in case of war with the United States.

            April 10. Han Si-dae, Kim Ho, and Song Jong-ik, delegates
            from the All-Korean National Association of North America,
            arrived in Honolulu to discuss current political situations
            with their counterparts from the Dongji-hoi and the All -Ko-
            rean National Association of Hawaii.

            April 20. The Conference of Koreans Abroad was held at the
            headquarters of the All-Korean National Association of Ha-
            waii. The delegates decided to create the United Korean
            Committee and to support the Korean provisional government-

in-exile with the "independence fund." Two-thirds of this
fund was earmarked for provisional government and the re-
mainder was to be sent to the Korean Commission in Washington, D.C. to support its diplomatic activities. The unity
among Koreans signified by the formation of the United Korean Committee was disrupted in 1943 when Syngman Rhee's
group, the Dongji-hoi seceded from the committee.

December 7. Japan made a surprise attack on Pearl Harbor.
During the attack, a Korean was killed.

On the evening of December 7, Korean residents in Los Angeles gathered together at the headquarters of the Korean
National Association and passed the following resolutions:
1. Koreans shall promote unity during the war and act
   harmoniously.
2. Koreans shall work for the defense of the country
   where they reside and all those who are healthy
   should volunteer for national guard duty. Those who
   are financially capable should purchase war bonds,
   and those who are skilled should volunteer for ap-
   propriate duties.
3. Koreans shall wear a badge identifying them as Koreans, for security purposes.

After the attack on Pearl Harbor, Colonel Hughes, the com-
mander of the California State National Guard, requested
the United Korean Committee to organize a Korean unit to
be incorporated into the California National Guard. On December 29, fifty Koreans, whose ages ranged from 18 to
64, were registered and began to receive military training.

1942   February 27-March 1. Under the auspices of the United
          Korean Committee, the Korean Commission, and the Korean
          American Federation, the Conference on Koreans' Freedom
          was held in Washington, D.C. A number of speeches and
          panel discussions were held during the conference which
          dealth with problems of Korean independence.

          March 1. The Korean unit attached to the California Na-
          tional Guard held the twenty-fourth anniversary of the De-
          claration of Korea's Independence in Los Angeles. After
          the ceremony, the unit held a military parade at Exposition
          Park.

          March 28. A ceremony launching the sale of the national

defense bonds was held at the War Memorial Hall in Pershing
Square Park. The day was designated as Korean Day, and
many people dressed in traditional Korean costumes participated in the ceremony.

May 4. Yi Jong-gun and Pak Yong-hak were commissioned
as Navy interpreters. They were sent to the Solomon Islands and later participated in the Guadalcanal campaign.
They returned to the U.S.A. on April 11 of the following
year.

May 10. The Korean unit attached to the California National
Guard came on a chartered bus from Los Angeles to San
Francisco in order to participate in a victory march. The
Korean flag was one of the twenty-seven national flags car-
ried by the marchers.

June 16. The North American Delegates Conference of the
Dongji-hoi was held in Chicago and many delegates from
Los Angeles, Montana, New York, and Chicago attended the
conference. At the conference, the delegates pledged to
support the Korean provisional government-in-exile.

August 29. A ceremony honoring the Korean flag was held
at the Los Angeles City Hall. After the ceremony, hundreds
of Koreans, as well as the Korean unit attached to the California National Guard, participated in a parade.

1943   The Puk-Mi Sibo, or the Korean American Times, was published by the Los Angeles branch of the Dongji-hoi in April
1943.

August 29. Koreans in Hawaii made a contribution amount-
ing to $26,265.35 to the U.S. government as a part of vic-
tory funds.

December 4. Military Order No. 45 was issued which ex-
empted Koreans from enemy alien status.

December 29. The Delegates Conference of the Korean National Association elected Song Hon-joo as chairman of the
Central Executive Committee.

1944   According to a report made on January 5, Koreans in America bought national defense bonds totaling $239,130 between
1942 and 1943.

February 12. The <u>Korean</u> <u>Pacific</u> <u>Weekly</u>, which had been
suspended after the Japanese attack on Pearl Harbor, received permission for publication from the military governor,
and Kingsley K. Lyu became editor of the weekly.

Early March. It was reported that the population of Koreans
in Washington, D.C. had increased since the outbreak of
the Pacific war. A total of thirty-seven Koreans were reported as residents of Washington, D.C. Of these thirty-
seven, five were college students, one was a middle-school
student and fouteen were college graduates who were employed by various governmental agencies.

April 14. Song Hon-joo resigned from the Central Executive Committee and Pak Won-gol was elected chairman of
the committee.

The United Korean Committee in America held an All Korean Leaders' Conference in October in Los Angeles. Syngman Rhee, chairman of the Korean Commission and stationed
in Washington, D.C., was ousted and Kim Won-yong was
chosen to replace Rhee.

The United States Post Office Department issued memorial
stamps on thirteen nations overrun by the Axis Powers.
The flag of each nation was printed individually on the
stamp. The thirteen nations whose flags were honored on
the stamps were Albania, Austria, Belgium, Czechoslovakia,
Denmark, France, Greece, Korea, Luxembourg, Nether-
lands, Norway, Poland, and Yugoslavia.

1945

January 2. It was reported that Kim Ho was elected chairman of the Central Executive Committee of the Korean National Association of North America.

March 10. Koreans in Honolulu established the Post-War
Assistance Society and began to collect relief goods amount-
ing to 700 tons. The relief goods were sent to Korea through
the American military government after Japan surrendered
on August 15.

August 30. Koreans in the continental U.S.A. established
the Post-War Assistance Society and began to send relief
goods. The society continued to operate until 1955.

October 16. Syngman Rhee arrived in Seoul, Korea.

A delegation representing Koreans in America was to be sent to Korea by the United Korean Committee. Due to certain administrative difficulties, the delegation was divided into two groups. The first group comprised of Han Si-dae, Kim Ho, Song Jong-ik, Kim Byong-yon, Kim Sung-nak, and Chon Kyong-mu left Hawaii on October 27 and arrived in Seoul, Korea on November 4.

1946 January 26. The second group of the delegation, composed of Kim Won-yong, Do Jim-ho, Ahn Kyong-song, Park Kum-wu, Choi Du-ok, Cho Je-on, Ahn Ch'ang-ho and Chong Du-ok, left Hawaii and arrived in Seoul, Korea on February 12.

August 4. Dr. Sammy Lee, a second-generation Korean, won an American national diving championship.

December 28. Paĭk Il-gyu arrived in Honlulu from the Mainland in order to work as editor of the Korean National Herald.

1947 January 1. It was reported that Yi Ok-hyong was elected chairman of the Central Executive Committee of the Korean National Association of North America, while Cho Byong-yo was elected president of the All-Korean National Association of Hawaii.

Philip Jaisohn, a naturalized U.S. citizen from Korea, returned to Korea on an invitation from the American military government in South Korea, arrived in Seattle. During his visit, he negotiated with a number of institutions of specialized and higher education to accept Korean students on scholarship.

August 24. A group of thirty-three Korean students, both male and female, arrived in San Francisco. They came to America to study at various institutions of higher education.

1948 January 2. It was reported that Dr. Kim Yong-song was elected chairman of the Central Executive Committee of the Korean National Association of North America.

The headquarters of the Dongji-hoi of North American held its convention and elected Yi Sal-um as its president.

August 15. The founding of the Republic of Korea with Syngman Rhee as its president was declared.

September 9. It was reported that there were 514,050 people in the Hawaiian Islands. Of these people, 5,570 were U.S. citizens of Korean ancestry, while 1,750 were aliens of Korean ancestry. Therefore, a total of 7,320 persons were of Korean ancestry.

September 25. Dr. Philip Jaisohn arrived in San Francisco. He was greeted by many Korean residents from various areas close to San Francisco.

The Republic of Korea established a consulate in Los Angeles and appointed Min Whui-sik as consul-general.

October 19. The Bureau of Immigration and Naturalization, Department of Justice, was requested by President Truman to delete a part of an order issued by the State Department in 1907 that prevented Korean and Japanese residents in Hawaii from coming to the Mainland.

1949   Syngman Rhee, president of the Republic of Korea, appointed Dr. Chang Myon, a graduate of Manhattan University, as Korean ambassador to the United States of America.

January 8. The Delgates Conference of the Korean National Association of North America was held in Los Angeles and Kim Ho was elected chairman of the Central Executive Committee of the association.

Kim Yong-sop, Korean consul-general in Honolulu, arrived to open the consular office.

May 2. It was reported that Nam Gung-yom was appointed as consul-general of New York, while Chu Yong-han was appointed as consul-general of San Francisco.

1950   January 2. It was reported that Kim Yong-sun was elected chairman of the Central Executive Committee of the Korean National Association of North America. He served in this post until the spring of 1961.

Various Korean organizations in Los Angeles worked together to invite to a dinner meeting fifty-six Navy officers from the Republic of Korea who had come to receive three destroyers transferred to the Korean Navy.

June 25. The Korean War started.

Kingsley K. Lyu, who had served as editor of the Korean Pacific Weekly, completed his unpublished manuscript, Korean Nationalist Activities in Hawaii and America, 1901-1945.

1951   January 5. Dr. Philip Jaisohn died at the age of eighty-three.

1952   January 18. A group of Navy officers from the Republic of Korea arrived in Seattle to undergo their naval training. They came to America to receive four destroyers transferred to the Korean Navy from the United States government. Various Korean social organizations worked together to entertain them at a banquet held on March 9.

April 17. A California court ruled that the Alien Land Law of 1913, which had been enforced for a period of thirty-two years, was unconstitutional.

April 25. The McCarran-Walter Immigration Act was passed by the House and was sent to the Senate for its approval. The Senate voted on the measure on June 10 and the act was later put into effect on December 24. The passage of the McCarran-Walter Immigration Act marked an end to the ineligibility of Oriental immigrants for American citizenship. It also established a quota system allowing a certain fixed number of immigrants to come to America from each nation.

1953   In order to commemorate the fiftieth anniversary of the arrivals of the Koreans in Hawaii, the Hawaii Korean Golden Jubilee Committee published a report, Fifty Years of Progress.

May 2 was declared Korean Day and Americans throughout the nation were encouraged to make donations in money and materials to help Korean refugees.

July 27. The armistice ending the Korean War was signed.

August 9. Ko Jong-ja, a representative of the Veterans' Association of the Republic of Korea, arrived in Los Angeles in order to raise money and materials to help veterans who were wounded during the Korean War. Many Korean residents in America responded to her plea by donating money and materials.

November 15-21. The fiftieth anniversary of the beginning
of Korean immigration to Hawaii was observed in Honolulu.
Ham T'ae-yong, vice president of the Republic of Korea, arrived in Honolulu to participate in the anniversary ceremony.
On the evening of November 14, a large group of Koreans
gathered together in a lecture hall of the Roosevelt High
School to welcome the vice-president.

The Korean Relief Society of Los Angeles made a contribution of $500 to Ko Jong-ja. It also made a contribution of
$1,207 to assist the Reverend Han Kyong-jik in his effort to
maintain and operate a home for the aged.

Early July. The Reverend Choi Yong-nong succeeded the
Reverend Oh Ch'ang-hi who had resigned as pastor of the
Korean Methodist Church of Los Angeles. The Reverend
Choi graduated from the Westminster Theological Seminary
in Philadelphia, where he received a Master of Arts degree
in 1950.

1954   April 9. A Korean choir arrived in San Francisco to raise
            a sum of ten million dollars to be used in educating war or-
            phans. The twenty-five members of the choir were orphans
            whose ages ranged from seven to twelve. Twenty-two girls
            and three boys were led by their advisor Chong Dal-bin.
            On Sunday, April 11, the choir visited the Korean Methodist
            Church of San Francisco and later left for Washington, D.C.

            July 26. Dr. and Mrs. Syngman Rhee arrived in Washington,
            D.C. They were greeted at the airport by Vice-President
            Nixon, John Foster Dulles, who was the secretary of state,
            General Ridgeway, who was the secretary of the army, and
            others. On July 28, he addressed the United States Congress,
            where he emphasized a close cooperation between the United
            States and Korea. He traveled to Los Angeles on August 3
            and was greeted by a large welcoming crowd. On August 7,
            he visited San Francisco where he stayed for two days. On
            his way back to Korea, he visited Honolulu.

1955   July 29. Chin P'il-sik, consul of the Korean consulate-gen-
            eral in Los Angeles, announced that Korean residents in
            America who wish to liquidate the independence bonds that
            they had bought since 1919, could not do so after August 15.

            September 22. It was reported that Mr. and Mrs. Chong
            Sung-gu and their family became the first Korean immigrants
            to arrive in the United States as war refugees.

1956   March 14-June 25. <u>Bohk</u> <u>Dohng</u>, a magazine of Hawaii's Ko-
                    reans, was published. Only seven issues of this fortnightly
                    magazine were published.

                    December 15. The Korean Students' Association in southern
                    California sponsored a traditional Korean play which was
                    accepted favorably by the audience.

1957   April 4. It was reported by the Korean government that a
                    total of 1,376 persons received exit permits to leave Korea
                    as emigrants during 1956 and 1957. Ninety percent of these
                    people declared North America as their destination.

                    April 5. It was reported that a Korean Baptist church was
                    established in Los Angeles. The Reverend Kim Dong-myong,
                    a graduate of the Southwestern Baptist Theological Seminary
                    with a B.D. degree, was appointed as the pastor of the
                    church. Mrs. Kim received an M.A. degree in the field of
                    religious education. The membership of the church was
                    approximately 100 persons, who made the church a self-
                    supporting institution. The church also planned to build a
                    nursery and a kindergarten.

                    May 1. The Korean Foundation was organized with Kim Ho
                    as its chairman. The purpose of the foundation was to pro-
                    mote higher education, scientific knowledge, and ideals of
                    democracy among Koreans in America. The following was
                    the platform of the foundation.
                    1. The foundation shall assist institutions whose efforts
                       are devoted to the development of the principles of
                       democracy and security of world peace.
                    2. The foundation shall serve as legal guardian for Ko-
                       rean students who wish to come to America for their
                       study and shall render financial assistance to students
                       who are unable to continue their study because of
                       their financial difficulty.
                    3. The foundation shall assist in publication of books
                       either written in English or in Korean which will con-
                       tribute to the further development of scientific know-
                       ledge.
                    4. The foundation shall engage in helping educational
                       and philanthropic enterprise only.
                    The founding members of the foundation made a $100 contri-
                    bution each, while Pak Yong-ha of Danube gave $1,000 to
                    the foundation. The Kim brothers donated a piece of prop-
                    erty estimated at $100,000.

June 13. Samuel Wilder King, Hawaii's territorial governor, appointed Herbert C. Choy as attorney general of Hawaii. He is the first son of Choy Du-ok, who came to Hawaii as an immigrant.

December 28. The Federation of Korean Students in America was organized with Paĭk Son-gi as its president. The purpose of the organization was to unite all Korean students studying in America into one organization.

1958   January 23. Mr. Harry Holt, a resident of Creswell, Oregon, arrived in Portland with eighty children who were born of Korean-American parentage. Mr. Holt had adopted eight children, and he had already brought to America five hundred Korean children who had been adopted by American families.

February 2. Ahn Ik-t'ae, the composer of the Korean national anthem, conducted the Burbank Philharmonic Orchestra. The audience applauded him for his outstanding performance.

June 15. A Korean student by the name of Paik Hak-jun delivered the valedictory at the commencement exercises at Stanford University. Never in its long history had Stanford University had a foreign student who delivered a valedictory.

June 20. It was reported that the Department of Education, Republic of Korea, recalled a total of 630 students who either completed their study or were failing their study. The Korean government decided to assist those who could not pay their own way by issuing $415 to each of them.

June 30. A Korean language school was opened at the Korean National Association building in Los Angeles. The school was to be opened to both boys and girls of six years of age and above, and it was to operate throughout the summer vacation on a five-day-a-week schedule.

The Federation of Korean Students in America launched a campaign to collect used books from American college and university students. Many Korean students in America participated in this drive for used textbooks to be sent to Korea for distribution among colleges and universities that were short of books in various fields. A total of 12,000 books were sent to Korea through this campaign.

July 27. The Reverend Kim Sung-nak who had worked for the last twenty years as pastor of the Korean Presbyterian Church of Los Angeles left for Korea. He was appointed president of Sungsil College, formerly known as Union Christian College.

December 27. The fiftieth annual delegates conference of the Korean National Association was held. Han Si-dae was elected president of the association.

1959

February 5. General Secretary of the Korean National Association C.H. Chang sent a letter to Mr. John Foster Dulles expressing his grave concern with the passage of the new National Security Law in South Korea.

March. Kim Won-yong, who once served as chairman of the Central Executive Committee of the Korean National Association of North America, published Chae-Mi Hanin o-simnyon-sa, or A Fifty-Year History of Koreans in America.

March 12. The House of Representatives of the United States passed, by 323 to 89, the bill to admit Hawaii as the fiftieth state. This was a significant event to many persons of Oriental ancestry who had been denied their U.S. citizenship.

March 21. The Korean National Association held an extra plenary session of the delegates and amended its constitution. The New Korea published the constitution of the Korean National Association in its issue of April 2.

March 22. A church service dedicating the education center of the Korean Presbyterian Church in Los Angeles was held.

April 2. Charles Ho Kim announced that Warren Kim's book A Fifty-Year History of Koreans in America was published and available for the people in the Korean American community.

The Korean Methodist Church building in Los Angeles was sold to the Greater True Light Missionary Baptist Church for $52,000. The members of the Korean Methodist Church decided to build a new church building with $72,000.

Danny Park, an eighth grade student at Walter Dexter School,

was the first place winner in the essay contest sponsored
by the Whittier Junior Women's Club. The complete text of
his speech was published in the May 14th issue of the New
Korea.

Richard Park, the second son of Park Young-sop, an elder
of the Korean Presbyterian Church in Los Angeles received
an M.D. from Marquette University.

May 14. President Eisenhower sent a special message to
the Korean Federation on the occasion of its establishment.

June 7. Mrs. Koh He-sung received a Ph.D. degree from
Harvard University. She is the wife of Dr. Koh Kwang-nim.

June 15. Mrs. Yang Je-hyon, wife of Yang Chu-eun, died
of a heart attack. She was born in Korea on November 11,
1896 and emigrated to the U.S.A. in 1913. She married
Yang on August 24 of the same year. She held many offices
during her lifetime. She served the Korean Women's Patriotic League as head of its San Francisco branch office.

The Korean Methodist Church that had sold its church building for $50,000 bought a lot at the corner of Virginia and
Washington in Los Angeles for a new church building.

The Reverend Peter Kwon was appointed minister of the Korean Presbyterian Church in Los Angeles by the presbytery
of Los Angeles.

Arthur Liem enrolled in electrical engineering at Harvey
Mudd College of Science and Engineering on two scholarships. He had been awarded both a California State Scholarship and a Harvey Mudd College Scholarship.

1960   January 14. Charles Ho Kim, chairman of the Korean Foundation, made a financial report. According to his report,
a total of $7,165 was spent on scholarship, while a total of
$700 was used as loans to students during the previous two
years.

March 17. Francis Whang, a pianist of Korean ancestry,
won a special award from Maestro Enrique Jorda, conductor
and musical director of the San Francisco Symphony Orchestra, to appear during one week of the 1960-61 season to perform for Maestro Jorda.

April 12. Alfred Song was elected to the city council of the city of Monterey Park. Song was the first person of Korean ancestry ever to be elected to a city council.

April 22. Kim Hyong-soon, chairman of the executive committee of the Korean National Association, called a meeting of the standing committee and briefed members on the political situation in Korea. The Korean National Association issued a resolution calling for a new election in Korea and for the release of those who had been arrested during the antigovernment demonstration.

April 23. A group of seventeen Korean students studying in San Francisco staged a demonstration in front of the consulate general office of the Republic of Korea protesting against the repressive measures used by the Korean government in its dealings with the antigovernment demonstrators.

April 24. Soprano Min Yong-whan gave a recital in the American Legion Hall in Beverly Hills. She received an M.A. in voice from Drake University in Iowa.

April 27. The Friendship Association of Washington, D.C. called an emergency meeting and formed the Korean Association of Washington, D.C.. Choi He-ch'ang was elected president of the association.

May 1. A mass meeting sponsored by the Korean National Association was held in the Danish Hall in Los Angeles. Three resolutions were passed at the meeting. One of them called for the establishment of a committee to promote unity among Koreans in America.

May 13. Charles Ho Kim, chairman of the mass meeting held on May 1, called a meeting of the Promotion Committee for Unity among Koreans.

June 7. Choy Bong-youn and his wife, both residents in Berkeley, California, received their resident certificate. They had been denied their certificate earlier because they had been suspected of being Communists. Choy later published a book, Korea: A History.

October 2. The Promotion Committee for Unity among Koreans was dissolved because representatives from various social and religious organizations from the Korean American community were unable to come to an agreement.

1961   Mrs. Elizabeth Kwon was invited to the Christian Education
          Leaders' conference by the Department of Christian Educa-
          tion of the United Presbyterian Church to be held at Newport
          Beach February 20 through February 24.

          Eight southwestern students were named as finalists in the
          1960-1961 National Merit Scholarship Program competition.
          Included among them were Nancy Woo and Penelope Choy,
          seniors at Manual Arts High School in Los Angeles.

          A display of Korean merchandise was on exhibit at the tenth
          annual Washington State International Trade Fair in Seattle.

          Penelope Choy was named as one of the Southern California
          winners of the National Merit Scholarship for outstanding
          academic achievement.

          Shin Byong-yul, a Korean Judo champion, began to teach
          the Japanese art of self-defense at Oklahoma State Univer-
          sity.

          Chong Du-ok, former president of the Korean-American
          Cultural Association of Hawaii and Washington, went to Ko-
          rea with his wife. He expressed his hope to publish his
          manuscript on the independence activities of Koreans in
          American during his stay in Korea.

          Pak Da-il was appointed by the Mutual Credit Bureau, a Los
          Angeles collection agency. He was the first Korean Ameri-
          can to enter this field. His appointment was made after a
          license had been granted by the State of California.

          Raymond Han of Honolulu, Hawaii was awarded an Opportun-
          ity Fellowship by the John Hay Whitney Foundation to further
          his art career. He was the fifth Korean American to win
          the award since 1948.

          A Korean pianist, Han Tong-il, a student at New York's
          Julliard School of Music, performed the Tchaikowsky Con-
          certo in D as soloist with the Detroit Symphony Orchestra.
          He was acclaimed last year for his playing of Liszt's Piano
          Concerto No. 1.

          Daye Shin, a former resident of San Francisco, opened his
          practice as attorney at law in Los Angeles.

The New Korea began to publish Daehan-in Kungmin-hoi
Yuksimnyon-sa, A Sixty-Year History of the Korean National
Association, by Im Ch'ang-mo. The first installment of
this serialized work was published on August 3.

The Korean National Association issued a statement that
plans were under way to encourage the participation of
Americans of Korean ancestry in the future activities of the
association.

The Berendo Street Baptist Church in Los Angeles celebrated
its second anniversary.

A Korean American team of four prominent public figures
from Hawaii left to survey conditions in Korea at first hand.
They were Barbara Kim, director of the Department of
Speech of the Hawaii Department of Education, Dr. Richard
W. Yoon, president of the Board of Regents of the University
of Hawaii, Robert W.B. Chang, a member of Hawaii State
House of Representatives and Herbert Y.C. Choy, former
attorney-general of Hawaii.

The Korean Chamber of Commerce of California was organized in Los Angeles. Frank Ahn was elected president
of the association.

Since the beginning of the membership drive for new younger
members, the Korean National Association signed up thirty-
two new members.

1962   January 6-7. The fifty-third annual delegates conference
            of the Korean National Association was held at the head-
            quarters of the Association.

            A committee for the Korean Community Center in California
            was formed at a dinner conference in Los Angeles. A
            standing committee was organized and Charles Ho Kim and
            Leo Song were elected chairman and vice-chairman, respec-
            tively. The Korean government was reported to have pledged
            a sum of between $25,000 and $50,000 toward the construc-
            tion of the center.

            Attorneys Daye Shin and Alfred Song of Los Angeles and
            Monterey Park, respectively, were appointed counselors
            to the Los Angeles Korean consulate.

A group of sixty persons of Korean ancestry met at the headquarters of the Korean National Association to launch a campaign to raise funds for the construction of the Korean Community Center. A total of sixty persons pledged to contribute $200,000 toward the project.

Six members of the Korean Women's Society of Hawaii made a visit to Korea to choose a project that could use $7,000 the the society had collected for a worthy cause.

The Founder's Medal of the Republic of Korea awarded to the late Ahn Ch'ang -ho was presented to Mrs. Ahn Ch'ang-ho in a ceremony in Los Angeles.

More than one hundred people attended the testimonial dinner in honor of Alfred Song, Monterey Park's vice-mayor and a candidate for the California State Assembly, on April 10 at the Pasta House in East Los Angeles.

Philip Ahn, a noted Korean actor and son of the late Ahn Ch'ang-ho, was made honorary mayor of Panorama City. Philip Ahn has appeared in over 200 movies and television films.

President Park Chung-hee of the Repbulic of Korea designated as part of his government's scholarship fund the $10,000 which had been donated by the Korean Women's Association of Hawaii.

June 7. David Paik of Whittier, California and Linda Lee of Reedley, California won the American Korean Civic Organization's scholarship prize of $50 apiece that is awarded annually to outstanding high school students of Korean ancestry.

Alfred Song of Monterey Park won the primary election for the Democratic nomination for the California forty-fifth district assembly seat.

The formation of Korea Institute, Inc., in Los Angeles was completed.

Edith Liem, daughter of Dr. and Mrs. Chan Liem of New Paltz, New York graduated from Vassar College. She was awarded the Frances Walker price as the senior showing the greatest proficiency in the study of piano.

Sonia Sok opened a business, Korean United Trading Company,in Los Angeles.

George Paik, son of the late Paik Il-kyu, received the degree of Doctor of Philosophy in bacteriology from the University of Southern California.

Miss Chong was employed to teach music in the Los Angeles County public school system. She was born in Korea and graduated with a B.A. and an M.A. in music from Cincinnati Conservatory and Florida State University, respectively.

December 21. A dinner party celebrating the election of Alfred Song to the California State Assembly was held.

December 29-31. The Korean National Association held its fifty-fourth annual delegates conference. Included in the agenda were the financial report for the year of 1962 and the decision to hold the annual conference of delegates between November 26 and December 5 of each year.

1963

January 24. The Reverend Kim Hyong-il resigned from his post at the Korean Presbyterian Church in Reedley, California and the Reverend Kim T'ae-yol succeeded him.

General Kang Young-hoon, former principal of the Korean Military Academy of the Republic of Korea, transferred from the University of New Mexico to the University of Southern California.

March 5. Mrs. Ahn Hye-yon, wife of the late Ahn Ch'ang-ho, left for Korea. She had been invited to visit Korea by the Korean government.

March 21. A group of six Koreans staged a demonstration in front of the White House protesting against the military government in Korea. Choi Kyong-nok, a retired general in the Korean army who once served as the chief of staff of the Korean Army, and others were involved in this demonstration.

April 5. The Korean Community Center was dedicated in Los Angeles.

April 10. Mrs. Ahn Hye-yon returned to Los Angeles after her thirty-five-day visit to Korea.

It was reported that the Young Men's Association of the Methodist Church was organized and Kim Kon-yong was elected chairman of the association.

April 19. Noh Sin-t'ae died. He was born in Korea and emigrated to Hawaii in 1902. In 1914 he moved to the mainland of the United States. He is the founder of the Oakland branch of the Korean National Association.

May 13. A ceremony commemorating the fiftieth anniversary of the founding of the Hungsa-dan was held at the headquarters of the Korean National Association. Dr. Chang Ri-wuk was a keynote speaker for the occasion.

May 17. It was reported that Miss Linda Lee, eighteen, a freshman at Reedley Junior College was crowned Reedley Princess at the ceremony commemorating the town's fiftieth anniversary.

June 7-11. Mr. Kim Se-yong, a noted Korean artist, held an art exhibit at the Korean Community Center.

It was reported that the University of California at Los Angeles graduated ten Korean students who received baccalaureate and advanced degrees. One of them received the degree of Doctor of Philosophy.

June 14. Lee Chae-jin, a postgraduate student and teaching assistant in the political science department at U.C.L.A., was elected president of the Korean Bruin Club.

Harvard University conferred the degree of Doctor of Philosophy on two Koreans. Kim Kyong-won received a Ph. D. in political science and Paik Je-hin received one in economics.

June 28. Chon Sil-yon won second place in the Asian Students' Tenth Essay Contest. Chon, who came to the United States in 1959, wrote "My Experience in America: An Evaluation."

July 12. It was reported that the valedictorian at the graduation ceremony of the Manual Arts High School in Los Angeles was Carol Sungjin Choi, the oldest daughter of the Reverend and Mrs. Choi Young-yong of the Korean Methodist Church of Los Angeles.

July 12. The New Korea launched a fund-raising campaign
jointly with the Kyonghyang Sinmun in Korea to help the
victims of Typhoon Shirley. A total of $415 was collected
during the first two weeks.

September 6. The University of California Press published
a book written by Cho Young-sam, Disguised Unemployment
in Underdeveloped Countries with Special Reference to South
Korea.

October 4. A young Korean artist, Kang Pyong D., held an
art exhibition at the Addison Gallery of Arts in Washington,
D.C.

October 11. It was reported that a comprehensive directory
of the Korean community in Southern California would be
published by the Oriental Heritage, Inc.

The University of California Press published a book by Lee
Chong-sik, The Politics of Korean Nationalism.

November 22. The Korean Student Association of the University of California at Los Angeles published the first issue of the Solim (Westwood).

December 6. A Korean student studying in Los Angeles
died in a Las Vegas hospital three days after he was stabbed
by a black in the Nevada resort. Noh Kook-chin, twenty-
five, a student at the National Technical School, was at-
tacked while trying to protect his wife.

December 6. Issues of "Vice of Korea," which had been
published between November 22, 1943 and March 1961, were
put together into a single volume by the Korean Affairs Institute in Washington, D.C.

1964   January 3. The New Korea announced that it would discon-
tinue free distribution of the paper to Korean students due
to financial difficulty. The New Korea had previously distributed approximately one hundred copies of each issue of
the paper to Korean students.

January 3. It was reported that the Korean Community Center was faced with a difficult financial crisis. Charles Ho
Kim, chairman of the board of directors, stated that the
financial crisis had been created mainly by those people

who had pledged to make a contribution but changed their minds.

January 17. The Taisung Club, a small social club at its inception, had grown to include forty members with a working capital of $8,000. The club heard Mr. J.F. Woodburn of Crowell, Weedon and Company, who spoke about investment strategies.

January 19. The fifty-fifth annual delegates conference of the Korean National Association was held at the headquarters of the association. Paik Jae-hyong and Han Jang-ho were re-elected president and vice-president of the association, respectively.

February 7. The Korean Education Foundation was established by a group of American citizens in cooperation with Union Christian College in Seoul, Korea. The foundation was established to promote the exchange of professors between Union Christian College and universities in the U.S.A., to invite Korean technicians and farmers for further education in the U.S.A., and to bring graduate students for short-term training.

February 7. The former president of the Republic of Korea, Syngman Rhee, was visited by his adopted son Rhee In-soo. In March, 1963, the former president had gone to Tripler Hospital in Honolulu for a physical checkup. He was later admitted to Maunalai Hospital and was reported as being critically ill.

February 14. The American Korean Civic Organization announced its program for 1964. The organization had been established five years earlier in order to help citizens of Korean ancestry to retain their cultural heritage. The program included art group activity, vocational guidance, social gatherings, golf tournaments, and invitations of prominent citizens to speak before members of the organization.

February 21. Gregory Kim, son of Mr. and Mrs. John Kim of Selma, California, won the 1963 scholastic award given to an excellent student by the American Korean Civic Organization.

February 28. Alfred H. Song, the first Korean American ever to be elected to a state legislature, announced his can-

didacy for reelection to the forty-fifth district assembly
seat of California.

March 6. Charles Ho-Kim, chairman of the Korean Foundation, announced that scholarships for Korean students
majoring in natural sciences were available. Any student
majoring in natural science, who maintained a grade point
average of "B" or better was eligible to apply for the $300
cas scholarship.

March 6. The Korean Community Center at its first executive meeting decided to hold a senior citizens' day in honor
of elderly citizens of Korean ancestry.

March 19. Richard Kim's The Martyred went through a fifth
printing. It was also reported that the best seller would
soon reach a total of 100,000 copies sold since its publication.

April 10. The Korean community directory was published
by the Oriental Heritage, Inc., in Los Angeles.

April 24. Chang Yu-sang, an assistant professor at Boston
University, became the first Korean to receive a doctoral
degree in business management. His Ph.D. dissertation
was "An Investigation of Stock Depletion Cost and Its Effect
on Inventory Control Models."

April 24. Kim Jae-kon, a resident of San Francisco, opened
a trading center called the Korean Import and Export Company,

Professor Peter Lee of the University of Hawaii published
an anthology of Korean poetry.

May 18. A Korean restaurant, Arirang, was opened in Los
Angeles.

May 22. Chang Dae-won, a professor at the Ken State University, received a Ph.D. degree from the University of
Michigan.

June 20. The National Gymnasium was opened in Los Angeles. It is operated by Koreans.

July 7. The summer classes of the Korean language school
sponsored by the Korean National Association were opened

to a group of thirty children, a majority of whom were second and third generation Koreans.

September 26. It was reported that Dr. Sammy Lee, a former American diving champion, was requested by the State Department to coach the Korean diving team at Tokyo, Japan.

October 2. Korean artists in Los Angeles decided to form an artists' association at a meeting held at the Korea House Restaurant.

October 9. The American Korean Civic Organization went on record as opposing Proposition 14 that was on the ballot of the November California general election. Proposition 14 was an initiative that sought an amendment to the California state constitution to give owners of peroperty in the state absolute discretion in the choice of a buyer or renter of their real property. Under the leadership of the American Korean Civic Organization, other Asian American groups formed a committee, Oriental Americans Against Proposition 14.

October 16. Yi Woo-keun, one of the outstanding tenors in Korea, was appointed the new choir director of the Korean Presbyterian Church in Los Angeles.

October 30. It was reported that Mrs. Nora Noh, a Korean dress designer, would open a brach shop in Waikiki, Honolulu, Hawaii.

November 6 . Alfred Song, the first Korean American ever to be elected to a state legislature, was reelected by a landslide, 43,773 to 27,433, over his Republican opponent.

November 15. A mortgage burning ceremony was held at the Korean United Presbyterian Church in Los Angeles to celebrate the successful mortgage fund raising campaign. The members of the church raised more than $4,750 to pay off the church's outstanding debts.

November 27. It was reported that Mrs. Syngman Rhee, wife of the ailing former president in exile in Hawaii, petitioned in a letter to President Park Chung-hee of Korea to bury her husband at the National Military Cemetery in Seoul after his death.

December 11. It was reported that the Reverend Don H. Kim, pastor of the Berendo Street Baptist Church, was elected vice-president of the Southern Baptist General Convention of California at its annual convention held at Long Beach.

1965

January 9. The Daisung Club held its annual meeting and elected Hyon Ch'ol as its president.

The second anniversary of the founding of the Korean Trade Center was observed in Los Angeles.

February 26. The Korea Foundation was moved from Reedley, California to Los Angeles. Also Kim Won-yong, author of The Fifty-Year History of Koreans in America, moved from Reedley to Los Angeles. It was reported that Kim would be in charge of the Korea Foundation.

May 18. The Reverend Whang Jae-kyong was awarded a medal by President Park Chung-hee of Korea during the latter's visit to the United States. The Reverend Whang had been very active in the affairs of the Korean community in America.

June 13. Pak Chung-soo and Yi Bom-jun, husband and wife, both received the Doctor of Philosophy degree in political science from the American University in Washington, D.C.

July 9. It was reported that the Korean Baptist Church in Los Angeles would establish a special English language class to serve those Koreans unable to speak English.

July 22. The Judiciary Committee of the House of Representatives passed a new bill that would do away with the restriction imposed upon emigration of Asians to the U.S.A.

July 27. The late Dr. Syngman Rhee was buried at the National Military Cemetery in Seoul, Korea.

July 31. Song Hon-joo died. He graduated from Roanoke College with a B.A. degree and later went to Princeton University, where he received an M.A. degree in 1917. He served the Korean Commission in Washington, D.C.

August 1. The Alumni Association of the Yonsei University was established in Los Angeles.

September 24. Ten graduates of the Korea University met at the Korea House Restaurant and decided to form the Alumni Association of the Korea University of Southern California in Los Angeles.

September 24. The Korean Bethany Church was established in Los Angeles. The Reverend Kim Hak-ch'ol was appointed minister of the church.

October 3. The new immigration bill was signed into law by President Johnson; it went into effect on December 1.

December 19. The Alumni Association of the Kyonggi Middle and High School was formed. Dr. Hong Ki-chung was elected president of the association.

December 28. The fifty-seventh annual delegates conference of the Korean National Association was held at the headquarters building of the association.

1966   January 8. The Alumni Association of the Korea University was established in Los Angeles, and Frank Shin was elected president of the association.

February 25. The Korean Church of Christ was established in Los Angeles and the Reverend Pak Kyu-hyon served the church as its minister.

The Southern California Branch of the Alumni Association of the Yonsei University established a scholarship to be awarded to students in Korea.

April 28. Hong Won-t'ak received a Ph.D. degree in economics at the age of twenty-five. It was said that he was the youngest person who received a Ph.D. degree in economics from Columbia University.

May 14. Radio Korea was discontinued after forty-nine weeks of operation. Radio Korea was established on June 10, 1965. Due to financial difficulty, Radio Korea was unable to continue its program.

May 29. A church service dedicating the Korean Christian Center was held in Los Angeles.

The Battle Memorial Institute began to recruit Koreans educated and trained abroad in the field of natural science to work for the Korea Institute of Industrial Technology and Applied Research.

August 7. The Reformed Korean Presbyterian Church was established in San Francisco.

The Korean American Foursquare Church was established in Los Angeles.

The Korean American Travel Agency established its Los Angeles branch office.

October 22. A benefit show was held in New York to raise money for the Children's Korean Language School in New York.

November 7. Yi Wha-soon Flower Shop was opened in Monterey Park, California.

December 11. The Korean Association of Southern California held its second annual meeting. Kim Ha-t'ae was elected president of the association.

1967   January 16. Paik Song-keuk opened his law business. He came to America in 1954 and studied at the University of Southern California.

January 27. It was reported that the Bank of Korea would establish its branch office in Los Angeles with the approval of the State of California in February.

March 5. A Korean church was established in Baltimore, Maryland.

March 5. The Dongji-hoi reorganized its organization. The chairman system was replaced by a committee system of seven persons.

March 28. Wui Sang-hak, an artist of high reputation in Korea, committed suicide in Los Angeles. Reasons for his suicide were not known.

May 1. Noh Jae-yon, author of A Concise History of Koreans in America, died of a heart attack. He was eighty-four years of age.

June 1. Kim Hak-hun was appointed editor of the New Korea.

The Korean American Chamber of Commerce of San Francisco was established.

June 27. Choi Jin-ha died. He was the eighth president of the Korean National Association. He came to America in 1916.

July 3. The Foreign Exchange Bank of Korea was established in Los Angeles. The name was changed to Korea Exchange Bank of January 1, 1968. Kim Yong-kwon was appointed director of the bank.

July 3. Im Ch'ang-mo, former chairman of the Board of Directors of the Hungsa-dan, died at the age of seventy-three. He was born in Korea on October 19, 1894. He left a manuscript on the history of the Korean National Association, "A Sixty-Year History of the Korean National Association," which was serialized and published in the New Korea.

Radio Korea resumed broadcasting by means of amplitude modulation. The program of Radio Korea had been discontinued due to financial difficulty.

August 18. Miss Kim Eva (Soon-hui) received a service medal from President Johnson for her outstanding service in Vietnam. She is presently working for Mr. Baunker, American ambassador to South Vietnam.

The Korea University conferred an honorary doctorate on Alfred Song.

September 22. The Alumni Association of the Hanyang University was formed in Los Angeles.

October 23. Kim Byong-yon, former general secretary of the Korean National Association died of a heart attack. He was born in Korea in 1893 and emigrated to the U.S.A. in 1913.

December 8. Chong Deung-nop, president of the Korean National Association, died of a stroke at the age of eighty-three. He came to America in 1905.

December 17. The fifty-ninth annual delegates conference

of the Korean National Association was held in the headquarters building of the association. Han Jang-ho was elected
president of the association.

1968   The Korean Youth Association was established in January.

January 5. Charles Ho Kim died. He was born in Korea on
May 25, 1884 and went into exile in October, 1912. He
came to the United States in 1914. He is the founder of the
Kim Brothers Company in Reedley, California.

March 10. The Korean Presbyterian Church and the St.
Paul Church in Los Angeles were merged and held a joint
service. Approximately 250 people attended the service.

April 15. Whang Yong-hun committed suicide. The reason
for his suicide was not known. He was attending school at
the time of his death. Whang graduated from Hankuk University of Foreign Studies.

July 18. Yi Am died. He was born in Korea on December
27, 1884 and came to America in 1903.

July 26. It was reported that a Korean church would be established in Sacramento, California.

November 8. The Korean Education Foundation was established in Los Angeles. Contributions made to this organization were tax exempt.

December 13. It was reported that the Korean Association
of Southern California would award the Kim Ho scholarship
to Korean students every year. Each student would receive
$100.

1969   January 10. The sixtieth annual delegates conference of the
Korean National Association was held at the headquarters
of the Korean National Association. Dr. Kim Sung-nak was
elected president of the association.

The Kim Ho Scholarship was awarded to three Korean students in Los Angeles. Each of them received $100. The
students who received the scholarship were Janet Wang,
Kwon Hui-ch'ang, and Kim Yong.

February 2. A ceremony marking the sixtieth anniversary
of the establishment of the Korean National Association was
held at the headquarters of the association.

February 14. The Reverend Wallen Lee was elected vice-
president of the California Presbyterian Synod, which
pleased and surprised the Korean community in America.
The Reverend Lee was twenty-seven years of age.

April 11. Mrs. Kim Dong-myong, whose maiden name is
Ahn Ee-suk, published If I Were to Die, I Will Die Gladly.

April 21. Mrs. Ahn Hey-yon, wife of the late Ahn Ch'ang-
ho, died.

June 9. The Hankook Ilbo, the Korean Times, began to publish its American news edition in Los Angeles.

July 1. Mr. Yi Byong-gan, who had served as general secretary of the Korean National Association, opened the Oriental
Service Center in Los Angeles.

August 8. It was reported that the Korean Women's Patriotic League made a contribution of $3,000 to the New Korea
for its continuing operation.

August 18. A group of sixty Korean residents in Washington,
D.C. staged a demonstration against the Korean government
for its attempt to amend the constitution of the Republic of
Korea to allow Park Chung-hee to run for the office of president for the third time.

September 5. The St. Paul Korean Church was changed to
the Pico Arlington Church. The Reverend Kim Yo-han (John)
was appointed minister of the church. The church was officially accredited by the Christian Churches of Southern California and Southern Nevada Area Board.

September 18. Mr. Jerry Lee, chief administrator of the
Panorama Hospital, was commended by the mayor of Los
Angeles, Sam Yorty. Jerry Lee was born on April 24 in
Los Angeles as the first son of Lee Byong-ok.

September 19. It was reported that the Campus Theatre in
Los Angeles would show Korean films twice a week.

October 24. It was reported that Whang Ch'ong-ha, a graduate of Columbia University, was elected president of the Philosophical Society of Detroit.

December 20. The sixty-first annual delegates conference of the Korean National Association was held at the headquarters of the association.

December 22. The Alumni Association of the Attached High School, College of Education, Seoul National University was organized, and Yi Wan-kyu was elected its president.

December 28. A church ceremony appointing four newly elected elders was held at the United Korean Presbyterian Church in Los Angeles.

1970   The North American Branch Committee of the Hungsa-dan held its delegates conference and elected Yi Ha-jon as its chairman.

January 10. The Alumni Association of the Attached High School, College of Education, Seoul National University held its first council meeting and passed a resolution to have the following activities: establishment of a scholarship, collection of books and publication of the association's magazine.

March 13. It was reported that Radio Korea would be broadcasting between 9 A.M. and 10 P.M. daily.

March 29. The Korean American Credit Union was established in San Francisco. The purpose of the organization is to promote the development of the Korean community in America.

April 16. Mrs. Martha Holt brought from Korea the five thousandth orphan who was adopted into an American family.

May 24. The United Association of the Young Korean Christians was organized at the United Korean Presbyterian Church in Los Angeles. Mr. Kim Sang-ki was elected chairman of the association.

June 15. Mr. Kwak Nim-dae left for Korea to reside there permanently. He spent half a century in the United States

working for the Korean community in America. He decided
to spend the rest of his life in Korea. He was eighty-five
years of age. He served as editor of the New Korea.

July 28. A group of eighteen young Koreans met at the Korea House Restaurant to promote the establishment of the
Korean Youth Association of Southern California.

October 3. The scholarship awarded every year to Korean
students in the United States by the American Korean Civic
Organization went to Miss Debra Lee this year.

November 20. It was reported that the New Korea Restaurant would be open for business on November 25 in Los
Angeles.

Sonia Sok, who runs a real estate business in Los Angeles,
donated a piano to Radio Korea.

1971   January 24. The Kim Ho Scholarship was awarded to five
Korean students. Each of them received $250.

January 24. The Korean Association of Southern California
held its annual meeting and elected Sonia Sok as its president.

February 12. Recent earthquakes in Los Angeles caused
financial losses for some Koreans. Several Koreans also
received minor injuries.

February 19. The Church of Nazareth was established in
Los Angeles by Han Soo-keun.

March 12. The Korean Temperance Society was organized
in Los Angeles. The purpose of the organization is to encourage Koreans not to smoke, not to drink beverages with
alcoholic content, and not to use narcotics.

March 19. It was reported that the Reverend Chang Si-wha,
minister of the Korean Central Church in Los Angeles, established the Los Angeles Theological Seminary.

April. The Seoul Food Market was opened in Los Angeles.

April 10. A ground-breaking ceremony was held at the Kimpo International Airport in Korea to build a control tower. Kim Si-myon, a Korean American businessman in Los Angeles, donated $50,000 toward the project. The tower will be named the Tower Dedicated to the Fatherland.

April 17. Korean Night was observed at the Academy of Motion Picture Arts in Los Angeles. A Korean film, Seven Princesses, was shown as a part of the program.

April 23. It was reported that a group of twenty-two Korean scholars in Buffalo, New York sent to President Park Chunghee a petition asking him to guarantee fair play in the coming general election in the Republic of Korea.

May 1. The Consolidated Tow Service was opened in Los Angeles to serve Koreans.

July 29. It was reported that the federal government made a grant of $50,000 to the chairman of the Asian American Social Workers Committee. The grant will be used in conducting research on social problems in the Asian American Community in Southern California.

August 8. The Korean Women's Patriotic League held its fifty-second anniversary, and approximately sixty members gathered together to commemorate the event.

August 12. It was reported that a total of 9,314 Koreans emigrated to the United States between July 1970 and June 1971.

August 19. It was reported that Mr. Edward Kim, son of Kim Sun-gol, graduated from Occidental College and was offered scholarships by six different colleges for advanced studies. He chose to go to the Medical School, San Francisco State University.

September 12. The Federation of Korean Church Musicians of Los Angeles was formed. The purpose of the organization is to promote church music. Cho Kwang-hyok was elected chairman.

October 7. The New Korea reported that Hobart School in

Los Angeles would offer English classes to Koreans unable
to speak English.

October 21. Mrs. Choy Chung-sook died. She was the
wife of Professor Choy Bong-youn, who was the author of
Korea: A History, published by Charles E. Tuttle Company
in 1971. Mrs. Choy was born in Korea in 1916. She studied at the University of California at Berkeley and wrote
a book on Korean cookery.

October 31. A public lecture was held under the auspices
of the Federation of Korean Church Musicians of Southern
California. Kim Byong-kon, professor at the California
State University at Los Angeles, spoke on the topic of
"Church Music and the Expression of Individual Faith."

November 6. The United Korean Presbyterian Church of
Los Angeles held its food bazaar. The proceeds will be
used to support the education of the children of Korean ministers.

November 6. The Korean Ministers' Conference of Chicago
was held at the First Korean Church in Chicago. The Reverend Kim Yan-guk presented his papers, "The Developmen-
tal Process of History as See from the History of Salvation."

November 14. The Friendship Association of the Korean
Ministers of Southern California held its meeting at the
Korea House Restaurant. The Reverend Cho Byong-soo,
an employee of the Los Angeles County Social Service Department, presented a paper, "Social Work in America."

November 19. The Korean Federation of Scientific and
Technical Managerial Personnel in America held its sym-
posium. The members heard Choi Sun-dal speak on the
"Present Situation of the electronic Industry in Korea and
Assistance that We Can Offer."

1972   January 8. The Korean Children's Choir of Los Angeles
             was organized.

             January 30. George Choi was elected chairman of the Ko-
             rean Association of Southern California.

             February 3. The Medical Health Service Center for Ko-
             reans was established in Los Angeles.

February 4. The Korean American Youth Foundation was established.

February 5. The Christian Counselling Center for Koreans was established in Los Angeles.

February 12. Jin Hyong-ki and Yi Kyong-dong were elected chairman and vice-chairman of the Board of Directors, Korean Association of Southern California, respectively.

February 17. The Korean American Cultural Association was established.

April 8. The first Miss Korean America was crowned.

April 22. The Korean Cultural Center was opened. The Korean language television station was opened in Los Angeles.

May 13. Mugung-wha Hakwon, or the Rose of Sharon Institute, was established in Los Angeles to teach young children of Korean ancestry the Korean language.

June 27. The Korean Food Products Manufacturers' Association of Southern California was established in Los Angeles.

June 30. It was reported that Korea had sent to the United States a total of 1,390 medical doctors to date. Korea was ranked third in the number of doctors who came to the U.S.A. from foreign nations. The Republic of the Philippines was first with its 3,003 doctors, while India was ranked second.

July 1. The Korean American Political Association of Southern California was organized in Los Angeles.

July 23. The Korean Women's Association of Southern California was organized in Los Angeles.

August. The Korean Philharmonic Orchestra was organized for the first time in the history of Koreans in America. The organization consisted of fifty members who were led by Cho Min-ku, who had once served as conductor for the Hollywood Philharmonic Orchestra.

August 24. Koreans launched a drive to send money to victims of floods in Korea.

September 3. A group of first generation Korean youth in Hawaii met to establish the Hangkuk Ch'ongnyong Yonhaphoi, or the Korean Youth Federation. The purpose of the federation was to unite all Korean youth organizations that exist in Hawaii. A person of Korean ancestry between eighteen and forty-five years of age was eligible.

September 19. The Korean Restaurants Association of Southern California was organized.

October 1. Moon Ch'ung-han was elected president of the Korean Association of San Francisco.

November 4. The Korean Academic Society and the Korean Association of Chicago held a conference to discuss various social and cultural problems with which Korean immigrants to America had been faced.

November 18. The American T'aekwon-do Association was organized in Los Angeles by thirty T'aekwon-do teachers who gathered in Los Angeles from various parts of the U.S.A. It was reported at the meeting that there were as of November, 1972, 700 T'aekwon-do institutes established in the U.S.A. All of them were reported as institutes where the Korean-style self-defense was taught.

November 26. The Korean Young Men's Christian Association was organized in Chicago.

December. The Athletic Association of Korean Residents in America was organized.

December 5. The Korean Cultural Center was granted the status of non-profit organization by the federal government.

1973   January 7. Kim Chong-sik was elected president of the Korean Association of Southern California. He was the sixth president of the association.

January 7. The first Korean Baptist Church was established in San Francisco. A group of eighty people attended the church service officiated by the Reverend Whang Im-ch'un.

The Berkeley Korean Presbyterian Church was established and thirty people attended the church service conducted by Yi Hyon-dal.

January 9. The governor of Hawaii, John A. Burns, signed a document declaring Korean Week between January 13 and January 17. The declaration was made to commemorate the seventieth anniversary of the Korean immigration to Hawaii.

January 14. The Korean Christian Church was established in San Francisco. A group of sixty people attended the first church service officiated by the Reverend Ch'on Byong-wook.

January 28. The first Korean Buddhist temple was established in Carmel, California. Four hundred people attended the ceremony dedicating the Sambo-sa, or the Sambo Temple.

February 3. The Dalma Temple was established in Los Angeles. A group of fifty people attended the first temple service.

February 4. A ceremony commemorating the sixty-fourth anniversary of the establishment of the Korean National Association was held at the headquarters of the Korean National Association. Yi Wha-mok, the president of the Korean National Association, presided over the meeting. One of the speakers, Dr. Kim Hyong-il, emphasized that the spirit of independence consists of self-reliance in politics, self sufficiency in economy, and spiritual freedom. He also stated that the independence movement and the spirit of independence would continue as Koreans had not achieved the three essential factors mentioned above.

February 10. The Korean Book Center was opened in Los Angeles. The proprietor of the bookstore was Kim Jin-hyong.

February 15. The Korean Residents Association was established in Santa Clara, California, and Kim Seung-un was elected president of the association.

February 21. The Korean Town Prosperity Association was established in order to push forward the plan to build a Korean town to be located along Olympic Boulevard, Los Angeles.

February 20. The One Day Service Center was established to help Koreans in Los Angeles solve their personal and social problems. The office of the Korean Association was used as the center.

March 3. Koreans in New York City selected Miss Korea to be sent to Korea to compete in the Miss Korea contest to be held in May.

March 18. Yi Dal-soon won the American ping-pong championship in Detroit where the championship competition was held. He was selected to represent the United States in the world ping-pong competition to be held in Yugoslavia in April.

April 14. The second Miss Korea of Southern California contest was held in Los Angeles, and Yi Hye-sook was chosen Miss Korea of Southern California. She was to be sent to Korea to compete in the Miss Korea beauty contest.

April 17. Noh Seung-jin, a second generation Korean, was elected to the board of education of Berkeley city. Noh was the first person of Asian ancestry to be elected to the Berkeley City Board of Education.

May 18. The Los Angeles County authorities appointed the Reverend Kwon Yong-bae as director of the Asian Community Service Center.

May 19. The Korean American Education Center was established in San Francisco. Im Yong-bin was appointed as principal of the center, which enrolled a total of seventy-three children of Korean ancestry. They were to receive instruction in Korean history, language, and culture. During the ceremony dedicating the center a number of Koreans mad financial contributions which amounted to $1,480.00.

May 20. A public ceremony commemorating the sixtieth anniversary of the establishment of the Hungsa-dan (Corps for the Advancement of Individuals) was held at the Sheraton-West Hotel, Los Angeles.

Yi Ch'ang-ho, a Korean resident in Silver Springs, Maryland, was arrested along with three Americans for violation of the Immigration Law and Labor Law. They were accused of having received a fee ranging from $200 to $1,500 from each prospective immigrant in Korea who subsequently received papers from the accused indicating that a job had been offered to him. These papers were, however, fabricated by the accused. Yi Ch'ang-ho was out on $5,000 bail.

May 20. A Korean church was established in Las Vegas. The Reverend Yu Kyong-il presided over the church service, which was attended by one hundred people.

June 25. The U.S. Supreme Court ruled that it was a denial of equal protection for a state to discriminate against aliens in providing state civil service employement.

July 1. A radio station broadcasting in Korean was established in Baltimore, Maryland.

July 21. The Korean Association was established in San Diego, California.

August 4. A group of children of Korean ancestry from Mu Kung-wha Hakwon, or the Rose of Sharon Institute, left for Korea to study Korean language, history, and culture. They were led by Kwon Kilsang, director of the Institute.

August 6. Kuk Young-il, former executive secretary of the Korean Association in Los Angeles, led a group of Koreans who staged a demonstration in front of the federal building in Los Angeles. The demonstration was staged in order to ask the authorities to facilitate the investigation of the Watergate incident. When asked, Mr. Kuk stated that the Watergate investigation should come to an end as soon as possible for the best interests of the American people.

August 7. Yi Ch'on-yong was appointed by Mayor Bradley of Los Angeles as one of 140 commissioners to serve the city.

September 8. A group of Korean residents in Chicago staged a demonstration led by Choi Myong-sang. The demonstrators wanted to restore a constitutional government in Korea.

October 28. The Korean Opera was organized in Los Angeles. Yi Woo-gun was elected president of the opera organization.

November 19. The U.S. Supreme Court ruled that a rejection of an application for employment by a private employer because the applicant is an alien is not a violation of the Civil Rights Act of 1964.

November 27. The Korean Association in Los Angeles was granted the status of non-profit organization by the State of California.

November 30. A hot-line service was opened for Koreans who may receive in time of need social services from the Korean community in Los Angeles. By December 14, the service center received 40 cases. An analysis of these cases indicated that Koreans had not been accustomed to the American way of life due to short history of their immigration, that they had language problems and a lack of understanding of how law functions in American society, and that family problems developed as results of their inability to cope with American culture.

December 20. The Korean Chamber of Commerce in Northern California was organized in San Francisco. Ch'u Ki-sik was elected president of the organization.

December 28. The Korean Association in Los Angeles was granted the status of non-profit organization by the federal government.

1974   January 12. According to a news release on this date, Professor Kim Bok-lim of the University of Illinois received a grant from the National Institute for Mental Health to study the community needs and problems of the Asian Americans.

January 12. Yi Hak-cho was elected chairman of the Korean Chamber of Commerce of Southern California. Also elected were thirteen people to serve on the board of directors.

The Society to Honor the Old-Aged and the Old People's Association were merged into the Korean Old People's Association, and Ahn Min-hong was elected president of the association.

The Students' Counciling Center of the Korean Students' Association of Southern California was established to offer free counseling to students in need.

January 19. According to a news release on this date Korean proprietors of a sauna business in Tacoma, Washington staged a protest against the attempt by the State of Washington to control and regulate their business by a state license system. There were as of January 19 a total of twenty-three sauna centers, and fourteen of them were owned by Koreans.

January 21. The Box Sales Company in San Francisco, owned by Ch'u Ki-sok, was burned down. The financial loss was estimated at $250,000.

January 21. The San Francisco Board of Education was ordered by a federal court to offer a special English language class to Chinese students who were at a disadvantage due to their lack of English language proficiency. This was a significant ruling in view of the fact that many children of Korean immigrant parents were faced with the same problem.

January 25. The Kim's Driving School was opened in Los Angeles by Kim O-hyon.

January 27. The annual conference of the Korean Association of Southern California was held at the Embassy Auditorium; 350 regular members attended to elect nine new members to the board of directors.

According to a new release, two Koreans passed the medical examination administered by the State of Nevada for Chinese medicine. Also, three Koreans apssed an examination that giave thema state license to practice acupuncture.

February 5. The California Microfilm Company began to microfilm Sinhan Minbo, the New Korea.

February 11. According to a news release on this date, a U.S. court of appeals handed down a unanimous decision supporting the eligibility of permanent residents for employment in the federal government. In view of the fact that most Koreans in America came to America in recent years, this decision was important for the economic and social well-being of the Korean American community.

February 17. The Federation of Korean Churches of Southern California held its annual meeting and elected Ahn Su-hun as its chairman.

February 19. The third edition of the telephone directory of the Koreans in Southern California was published by the Hankook Ilbo of Los Angeles.

February 21. The Seoul Choir was organized.

February 24. Yi Min-whui was elected president of the Korean Association of San Francisco. Also elected were ten members of the board of directors.

February 26. The Research Association of the Koreans in America was established, and Kuk Young-il was elected chairman of the association.

March 6. According to a news release on that date, the rate of unemployment among Koreans in Southern California had increased. It was reported that approximately 22 percent of the Koreans in Southern California was unemployed.

April 1. According to a news release on that date, a total of thirty-seven Korean nurses passed the California State Registered Nurse Examination.

April 3. According to a news release on that date, the Board of Education of Los Angeles decided to hire several Korean teachers who would be working with Korean children with language difficulty.

April 25. Breed University was established in Los Angeles by Ko Ung-ch'ol, a Korean resident in Japan. The university was established to promote the World Unity Movement. It was reported that the university would offer courses in Korean, English, French, German, and Japanese.

HORACE ALLEN'S LETTER TO SANFORD B. DOLE, GOVERNOR OF HAWAII
1902

The Reverend Horace N. Allen wrote this letter to the governor of Hawaii, Sanford B. Dole, in an attempt to explain the social, economic, and political conditions that had forced the Korean government to ease the restriction imposed on the emigration of Korean people to other parts of the world.

Source: Archives of Hawaii, Governors' Files, Dole-Foreign Officials, Including Consuls A-M.

His Excellency,
Sanford B. Dole,
Governor of Hawaii,
Honolulu, H. I. (Received January 13, 1903)

Sir:

I take the liberty of handing you duplicate copies of an edict recently issued by the Korean Government regulating the emigration of Korean subjects to foreign countries.

My reason for sending you these copies is that I learn it is the intentions of a number of Koreans to try the experiment of emigrating to Hawaiian Islands during the coming winter, with the idea of bettering their conditions and preparing the way for others to follow in case the conditions are found to be satisfactory.

Heretofore it has been somewhat difficult for Koreans to get permission to leave their country, without which permission emigration would be attended with trouble on returning to their native land. The severe famine of the past winter made the matter seem all the more attractive to the people, while the fact that the Government had to import large quantities of rice to feed the starving seems to have turned the attention of the officials favorably to the subject of emigration. It is probable however that the pride of the Emperor in learning that his people might go where the great Chinese are excluded, had much to do with the matter.

The Koreans are so poor that not many of them would have the necessary funds without borrowing, for the purpose of emigrating with their families, but I am not at all inclined to think that this Government has any intention of assisting its people to emigrate by advancing them the necessary funds. On the contrary, it is probably their intention of profiting from the people on their return. I imagine that those who are accompanied by their families may not care to return if the conditions are favorable to their residence abroad.

The Koreans are patient, hard-working, docile race; easy to

control from their long habit of obedience. They are usually very keen on getting a foreign education, and this has taken quite a number to the United States where a few have become naturalized, while those who have returned are doing well and are a credit to their American education.

Koreans have emigrated to Siberia in considerable numbers and they are reported as being most prosperous there where they are relieved from the official oppression which curses their own land.

It may be that these pioneers, if they actually get off, may not find the climate of Hawaii suitable to them, though they seem to thrive well in Japan, where colonies have lived for some centuries. The Koreans taught the Japanese the art of making pottery and the original colonies are still intact in Japan, due to the regulations of the Japanese Government regarding them.

The Koreans are a more teachable race than the Chinese; they eat more meat than do the latter people, though their chief article of diet is rice.

If Koreans do get to the Islands in any numbers it will be a God-send to them (Koreans) and I imagine they will be found to be unobjectionable and of good service as laborers.

> I have the honor to be, Sir:
> Your obedient servant
> Horace N. Allen (signed)

DAVID W. DESHLER'S LETTER TO HUNTINGTON WILSON
1906

David W. Deshler was an agent sent to Korea by an overseas development company to recruit Korean laborers. When the Korean government put an end to the emigration of Koreans to the Hawaiian Islands under the political pressure of Imperial Japan, he wrote this letter to Huntington Wilson, Charge d'affaires, American Legation, Tokyo, Japan, asking him to intervene on his behalf and to influence the Japanese government so that the Korean emigration may be renewed. This letter was enclosed in a letter of Huntington Wilson, dated January 27, 1906 to Elihu Root, Secretary of State.

Source: Archives of Hawaii, Governors' Files, Carter -- U. S. Depts. October 1905 -- June 1907.

Sir:

I beg to intrude on your valuable time for the purpose of setting forth the history and present conditions of matters relating to the emigration of Korean laborers from Korea to the Hawaiian Islands.

This work was organized after many failures and great difficulty, and the first emigrants left Korea on the 22nd of December 1902. From that time until the early part of April 1905, the work went on without serious interruption and a total number of some seven thousand men, women and children emigrated to Hawaii to engage in work on the sugar plantations there.

On or about the 4th day of April, in the year 1905, an order was given under the name of the Korean Government, but with the consent and advice of His Excellency, the Japanese Minister to Korea, prohibiting the further emigration of Koreans, no matter what their destination might be.

On receipt of these advices the writer immediately went to Seoul and there had an interview with the Foreign Minister, Mr. Yi Ha Yung, and in reply to the protest made by the writer, Mr. Yi gave the following as his reason for taking the action he had.

That personally he was greatly in favor of the emigration to Hawaii, that he knew the management of the Company who represented the Territorial Bureau of Immigration in Korea had the reputation of having always safeguarded the interests of the emigrants in every way possible and that they had been treated with kindness and consideration; that he personally recommended and advised many Koreans to go to Hawaii, some of whom had taken the advice and had done well in their new field of labor; that on the whole he had not one single objection to offer to Korean emigration to Hawaii, but on the contrary was most strongly in favor of it.

He said that the reason for the stopping of the emigration was the fact that there had recently come to Korea a new irresponsible company, who, by promise of high wages and other advantages, had induced some nine hundred Koreans to take passage on a vessel especially chartered to convey them to Mexico; that the management of this new company did not meet with their approval, that they had misrepresented his views and opinions in the matter of the Korean emigration to Mexico, and that he did not consider Mexico a suitable place for Koreans to go to in any numbers; and inducing them to emigrate to undesirable places by irresponsible people, and that in order to effectually stop this undesirable work, he originally intended to prohibit the emigration of Koreans to Mexico, but that upon consultation with His Excellency, the Japanese Minister to Korea, the Japanese Minister pointed out that it would be unfair to discriminate in favor of any emigration company or country, and that if one were stopped, all must stop.

Mr. Yi then concluded that it was the easiest way out of the difficulty and the way best calculated to protect the interests and rights of his people to stop emigration entirely until such a time when laws and regulations could be drawn up and put in operation which would offer emigrants the desired protection.

The writer pointed out to Mr. Yi that the work which had developed on the writer of sending emigrants to Hawaii was one which had been in operation for several years; that several thousand Koreans had already gone to Hawaii, and that the features of Hawaiian emigration were known to all, and that it had the approval of the Korean officials, the Korean people and foreigners generally, and of the majority of the missionaries, who saw in the work an opportunity for Koreans to improve their condition and to acquire useful knowledge and to better themselves financially.

Mr. Yi replied that he was perfectly aware of this and that no one had any objection to Hawaiian emigration, and that it was a question of discrimination and he asked the writer to stop the work until such a time as the rules and regulations contemplated could be put into effect. This the writer did, and with the exception of a few men who had left their homes in the interior of Korea and gone to seaports ready to embark, no one left the country for Hawaii.

The writer pointed out to Mr. Yi that he would personally be very glad to work under such rules and regulations as the Korean Government saw fit to enact to protect their countrymen and that the enforcement of the same would have his fullest sympathy and support. The writer further pointed out to Mr. Yi that as a mark of confidence he has received a document from the Emperor of Korea authorizing him to take charge of all emigration matters in Korea, and that while the writer had the right to appeal from the order of the Foreign Office as directly interfering with the rights granted him by the Sovereign he much preferred to work in harmony with the Government and not put any obstacles in the way of the enactment and enforcement of laws which he himself deemed to the best interests of the Koreans.

A period of nine months now having elapsed, it would seem that ample time had been had to have investigated emigration conditions and to have enacted suitable laws and regulations by which emigration could be carried on. The delay and interruption that this work has had has been of great financial loss to me, and I have the honor to request that you will be kind enough to make such representations to the authorities at Tokyo as may seem best likely to tend to an early revival of this work. The document which the writer holds, and of which he begs to enclose you a copy and translation herewith, confers on him certain rights and privileges which he has been prevented from enjoying in the past nine months. It is the writer's firm belief that there is no objection on the part of the Imperial Japanese Government to the emigration of Koreans, properly regulated, and the writer will be very glad to comply with any reasonable regulations which the Imperial Government may see fit to impose.

Begging for the above your kind consideration,

I am, Sir,
Respectfully yours,
D.W. Deshler

THE KOREANS IN HAWAII
1906

American missionaries encouraged Koreans to emigrate to the Hawaiian Islands. Of all American missionaries who had some influence upon the Korean emigrants, the Reverend George Heber Jones, the author of this article, was most influential. He helped Koreans ready to embark upon their ships for a long voyage to an unknown land by giving letters of introduction to some of their leaders. Later when he came to the Hawaiian Islands, he visited various work camps of the Korean emigrants.

Source: George Heber Jones, ''The Koreans in Hawaii,'' Korea Review, VI, 11, November 1906, pp. 401-406.

Hawaii, one of the beautiful portions of the earth's surface, presents one of the most vividly interesting yet tragic chapters of history to be found in human annals. For centuries the home of a generous, proud Island race, its original owners are fast vanishing away and other races have entered upon their inheritance. One is impressed with this as he moves about the Islands. Instead of the brown Kanaka, sturdy of physique and generous and happy-go-lucky in character, Japanese, Chinese and Koreans alternating with Portugese and Puerto Ricans meet the eye everywhere. The population is highly cosmopolitan in character, with the Asiatic in the lead.

From January 1903 to December 1905, 7,394 Koreans found their way to the Islands, of whom 755 were women and 447 were children under 14 years of age. The emigration ceasing about this time very few have gone there since. The departures have been very small in number so that probably eighty per cent or about 5,700 Koreans must be still residing in the Islands. Of those who have left the Islands, three-fourths have gone on to the Mainland where they may be found in large cities like San Francisco, Oakland, Los Angeles, and Pasadena working as house servants; or in the country districts of California as laborers on the fruit farms; they are on the cattle ranches in Wyoming, for the Korean abroad takes naturally to horses and owns one for himself as soon as possible. They are down in the corn belt, and may be found working as track hands along the Union Pacific and Southern Pacific Railroads.

It is in Hawaii the Korean is at his best. At first he had some difficulty in adjusting himself to his surroundings. Everything was new and strange and he had to learn how to handle himself. He did not know how to live, but it did not take him long to learn how to do so. He had to learn what to wear and where to get it, what to eat, where to buy it, and how to cook it; how to work and how to take care of himself. The Korean, when placed in favorable circumstances, is wonderfully quick to learn and in a marvelously short length of time, he learned his lessons and today the universal testimony is that the Korean is a very desirable plantation hand.

To understand the circumstances surrounding the Korean in Hawaii, it is necessary to understand one thing -- sugar. The Korean's whole experience is wrapped up in that one word. Sugar is the keynote to everything in Hawaii. Nature has so ordained it. "Directly or indirectly all industries in Hawaii are ultimately dependent upon the sugar industry -- the social, economic and political structure of the Islands alike are built upon a foundation of sugar." The total value of exports from Hawaii for the year ending June 30, 1905 was $35,123,867 and of this amount, sugar represented $35,113,409.

Hawaii is a land of surprising limitations. From the above, it will be seen that it is a land of practically one crop, the entire population being dependent virtually on this one industry. The superficial land area of the Islands is only about 6,000 square miles and of this, it is estimated that only one-tenth is arable, giving us only about 600 square miles to provide sustenance for the entire population of these islands. This area is divided into a few great plantations, some of them containing thousands of acres stretching for miles along the coast, employing a small army of laborers and producing as high as 45,000 tons of sugar on a single plantation.

Employed in producing this great crop are 48,229 -- divided according to the following percentage (1905).

Japanese	65.80
Chinese	9.14
Korean	9.71
Portugese	6.23
Hawaiian	3.01
Puerto Rican	3.95
Caucasian	2.09
Negro, South Sea Islanders	.07
	100.00

From this it will be seen that the Koreans rank second in numbers on the sugar plantations, and play no small part in the production of Hawaii's great crop. It is further interesting to note the distribution of Koreans on the Plantations according to occupations.

Administration	10
Cultivation	4,384
Irrigation	1
Manufacture	19
Superintendence	4
Transportation	248
Unclassified	17
	4,683

By administration is meant clerks, interpreters and the like. Only one Korean is down as working at irrigation. This is one of the most expert forms of farm labor and though more Koreans are at work now at it, for I personally knew of a gang of twenty of them who were doing fine, yet it is doubtful if they will ever play a large part in this as irrigation is done largely by Japanese who are regarded as unexcelled at it. In the work of manufacture, an increasing number of Koreans are being taken into the mills, while some, a very few, have been taken into the engine room of certain mills and started out as firemen and machinists. Very few have been employed as lunas or bosses though I met several of whom their bosses spoke very highly, but most of the Koreans work under white or Hawaiian bosses, either in gangs by themselves or in mixed gangs alongside Japanese, Puerto Ricans and Portugese.

From this, it will be seen that about severty-five percent of the Koreans are at work on the plantations. The balance is made up of the women -- for as a rule the Korean women are not compelled by their husbands to work in the fields; the children who are compelled to go to school; the store keepers and inn keepers; the students and the floating population in Honolulu.

The Korean field hand receives $18 a month in U.S. gold for twenty-six days of labor. No Sunday labor is required, everything being shut down on the plantations on the Sabbath. If he has a family, he is given a house to himself with a little garden patch. Fresh clean water and fuel are supplied gratis, and the hospital with a trained resident physician is always open to him. Schools conveniently located, with American teachers, furnish education in English for his children. In the larger settlements like Ewa, a school in Korean, taught by a Korean schoolmaster, is maintained by the Koreans themselves.

If the Korean is unmarried, he is assigned to a dormitory with other Koreans, the number being strictly limited by law to the cubic contents of the house. Sanitary inspection is both frequent and rigid and the Korean has learned to understand its value. Actual living expenses vary from $6.00 to $9.00 a month. This diet usually consists of rice with vegetable salad, meat, soup, and bread and butter. The Koreans eat much fruit, especially the papaya and the pineapple and more recently, have taken to American tinned provisions. In visiting their camps, I had many a meal with Koreans which though homely, was well cooked and as good as any man might wish. As a rule, the Koreans live well. They wear American clothing, eat American food, and act as much like Americans as they can.

The Korean gets his breakfast about four o'clock in the morning and by five o'clock he is in the field at work. If it is some distance to his field, he is carried on the plantation railroad back and forth. Quite a number of the Koreans own their own horses and ride back and forth. This is true of the bosses, interpreters and Korean business men. A little incident will illustrate this.

I arrived at Mokuleea earlier than was expected so there was no one to meet me. My Korean companion told me there was a Korean store kept by a Christian a little distance away and we could get a horse there. On arriving at this store, what was my surprise to find a young man and his family whom I had baptized and taken into the church in Korea some years before, running this store and happy and prosperous. After the surprise and pleasure of the meeting, he quickly hitched up his horse and wagon, drove me to the camp two miles away, hastened back for his wife and baby born a few months before on American soil, and thus a future American citizen, and that night in the little chapel erected by the Koreans themselves I baptized the baby with several adult Koreans.

The Korean's day in the field is ten hours. He takes his lunch with him and eats it in the field. He gets back to camp about 4:30 P.M., usually takes a hot bath, puts on clean clothes, and is ready for supper and the evening.

One third of all the Koreans in Hawaii are professing Christians. They dominate the life in the camps on the Islands of Oahu, Kauai and Maui where they are stamping out gambling and intoxication. The Korean has fallen into sympathetic hands in Hawaii. The Sugar Planter's Association is composed of gentlemen of the highest character and integrity, genuinely interested in the welfare of their hands and ready to cooperate in every sensible measure that promises better things for their men. There is a total absence of the "Jim Crow" spirit in Hawaii and the good nature with which the various races mix there is wonderful. On the railroads and steamers, they crowd and jostle each other but no one ever complains and all nationalities stand an equal show. A Chinese or a Korean, if he puts up the money, can travel first class and receive as much attention as any other nationality. There is a kind-hearted, gentle and generous spirit in everything in Hawaii that is delightful.

Under such conditions the Korean grows and develops very rapidly. Hawaii is the land of great possibilities for him. Being a farm laborer, he gets the very training he needs to fit himself for usefulness in his native land. Hawaii becomes to him a vast School of Agriculture where he learns something of the character and treatment of different soils; methods of irrigation and fertilization; care and system in the handling of the crops. He learns how to work according to system, and also the value and obligation of law and regulation. If a thousand selected Koreans a year could be permitted to emigrate to Hawaii in a few years, they would return and develop the natural resources of Korea, adding many fold to the value and financial resources.

RESOLUTION OF THE CONFERENCE OF THE
UNITED PROMOTERS
1907

This resolution was adopted on September 2, 1907 by the representatives of twenty-four Korean organizations established in
various parts of the Hawaiian Islands.

Source: Won-yong Kim, Chae-Mi Hanin osimnyonsa, Reedley,
California: Charles Ho Kim, 1959, p. 96.

Article 1: We are united in our strength to assist activities aimed at
the restoration of the sovereignity of our fatherland, to secure
the welfare of the Korean residents in Hawaii, and to promote
educational works.

Article 2: Various organizations established in different parts of the
Hawaiian Islands shall be united into an organization called the
Hapsong Hyophoi, or the United Federation, and its headquarters
shall be located in Honolulu. All other organizations established
in different parts of the Hawaiian Islands shall be abolished and
branch offices of the United Federation shall be organized.

Article 3: The headquarters of the United Federation shall send its
supervisors to various regions to explain reasons for unity to
those organizations and individuals that have not joined the Federation.

Article 4: The United Federation shall publish its organizational newspaper to be called the Hapsong Sinbo, or the United Herald. All
other newsletters previously published by various organizations
shall be incorporated into the United Herald in order to promote
unity.

THE STATEMENT OF THE UNITED PROMOTERS
1908

The representatives of the United Federation of Hawaii and those of the Mutual Cooperation Federation of North America made an agreement to merge the two organizations and to create the Korean National Association. This was the first united organization in the United States proper to coordinate various efforts of Koreans in their struggle for national independence.

Source: Won-yong Kim, Chae-Mi Hanin osimnyonsa, Reedley, California: Charles Ho Kim, 1959, p. 102.

Complying with the needs of time and the public opinion, we have drafted a resolution with seven articles in order to unite the United Federation and the Mutual Cooperation Federation into one organization for the purpose of mutual assistance. We hereby declare that we have agreed to unite the two organizations as soon as they pass the resolution.

Article 1: The Mutual Cooperation Federation of America and the United Federation of Hawaii shall disband their organizations and be united into one organization which shall be known as the Korean National Association.

Article 2: The date of unity shall be February 1, 1909.

Article 3: Each organization shall elect three members to serve on the Rules Draft Committee, and they shall develop through discussion rules for the Korean National Association.

Article 4: The place of conference for the Rules Draft Committee shall be determined by two organizations in consultation.

Article 5: The rules of the Korean National Association shall be based on the principles of democracy.

Article 6: The existing rules shall be enforced until the new rules go into effect.

Article 7: The present authorities shall manage business until new officers of the united organization are appointed.

November 30, 1908

Representatives of the United Federation of Hawaii: Ko Sok-ju, Kim Song-kwon, Min Ch'an-ho, Yi Nae-soo, Kang Yong-so, Han Jae-myong, and Ahn Won-kyu.

Representatives of the Mutual Cooperation Federation: Choi Chong-ik, Yi Dae-wi, Kang Yong-dae, Ahn Sok-jung, Whang Sa-yong, and Yi Kyong-ui.

DECLARATION OF INDEPENDENCE
1919

This Declaration of Independence was originally written in Korean by Choi Nam-son. On March 1, 1919, the declaration signed by the thirty-three representatives of various social, religious and cultural organizations in Korea was proclaimed in Seoul. Koreans in America received the news of the March first demonstrations when the cablegram, dated March 1 and signed by Hyon Sun in Shanghai, was received by Ahn Ch'ang-ho on March 9. During the First Korean Congress, held on April 14-16, 1919 in Philadelphia, Syngman Rhee read the Declaration of Independence in front of Independence Hall.

Source: F.A. McKenzie, Korea's Fight for Freedom, New York: Revell, 1920, pp. 247-250.

We hereby proclaim the independence of Korea and the liberty of the Korean people. We tell it to the world in witness of the equality of all peoples and we pass the principle of national self-determination on to our posterity as their inherent right.

We make this proclamation, supported by 5,000 years of history and by 20,000,000 united loyal people. We take this step to insure to our children for all time to come, personal liberty in accord with the awakening consciousness of this new era. This is the clear leading of God, the moving principle of the present age, and the just claim of the whole human race. It is something that cannot be stamped out, or stifled, or gagged, or suppressed by any means.

Victims of an older age, when brute force and the spirit of plunder ruled, we have come after these long thousands of years to experience the agony of ten years of foreign oppression, with every loss to the right to live, every restriction of the freedom of thought, every damage done to the dignity of life, every opportunity lost for a share in the intelligent advance of the age in which we live.

Assuredly, if the defects of the past are to be rectified, if the agony of the present is to be unloosed, if the future oppression is to be avoided, if thought is to be set free, if right of action is to be given a place, if we are to attain to any way of progress, if we are to deliver our children from the painful, shameful heritage, if we are to leave blessing and happiness intact for those who succeed us, the first of all necessary things is the clear-cut independence of our people. What cannot our twenty millions do, every man with sword in heart, in this day when human nature and conscience are making a stance for truth and right? What barrier can we not break, what purpose can we not accomplish?

We have no desire to accuse Japan of breaking many solemn treaties since 1636, nor to single out specially the teachers in the schools or government officials who treat the heritage of our ancestors as a colony of their own, and our people and their civilization as a nation of savages, finding delight only in beating us down and bringing us under their heel.

We have no wish to find special fault with Japan's lack of fairness or her contempt of our civilization and the principles on which her state rests; we, who have greater cause to reprimand ourselves, need not spend precious time in finding fault with others; neither need we, who require so urgently to build for the future, spend useless hours over what is past and gone. Our urgent need today is the settling up of this house of ours and not a discussion of who has broken it down, or what has caused its ruin. Our work is to clear the future of defects in accord with the earnest dictates of conscience: Let us not be filled with bitterness or resentment over past agonies for anger.

Our part is to influence the Japanese Government, dominated as it is by the old idea of brute force which runs counter to reason and universal law, so that it will change, act honestly and in accord with the principles of right and truth.

The result of annexation, brought about without any conference with the Korean people, is that the Japanese, indifferent to us, use every kind of partiality for their own, and by a false set of figures show a profit and loss account between us two peoples most untrue, digging a trench of everlasting resentment deeper and deeper the farther they go.

Ought not the way of enlightened courage to be to correct the evils of the past by ways that are sincere, and by true sympathy and friendly feeling make a new world in which the two peoples will be equally blessed?

To bind by force twenty millions of resentful Koreans will mean not only loss of the peace forever for this part of the Far East, but also will increase the every-growing suspicion of four hundred millions of Chinese -- upon whom depends the danger or safety of the Far East -- besides strengthening the hatred of Japan. From this all the rest of the East will suffer. Today Korean independence will mean not only daily life and happiness for us, but also it would mean Japan's departure from an evil way and exaltation to the place of true protector of the East, so that China, too, even in her dreams, would put all fear of Japan aside. This thought comes from no minor resentment, but from a large hope for the future welfare and blessing of mankind.

A new era wakes before our eyes, the old world of force has gone, and the new world of righteousness and truth has come. Out of the experience and travail of the old world arises this light on life's affairs. The insects stifled by the foe and snow of winter awake at this same time with the breezes of spring and the soft light of the sun upon them.

It is the day of the restoration of all things on the full tide of which we set forth, without delay or fear. We desire a full measure of satisfaction in the way of liberty and the pursuit of happiness, and an opportunity to develop what is in us for the glory of our people.

We awake now from the old world with its darkened conditions in full determination and one heart and one mind, with right on our side, along with the forces of nature, to a new life. May all the ancestors to the thousands and ten thousand generations aid us from within and all the force of the world aid us from without, and let the day we take hold be the day of our attainment. In this hope let us go forward.

Three Items of Agreement

1. This work of ours is in behalf of truth, religion and life, undertaken at the request of our people, in order to make known their desire for liberty. Let no violence be done to anyone.

2. Let those who follow us, every man, all the time, every hour, show forth with gladness this same mind.

3. Let all things be done decently and in order, so that our behavior to the very end may be honorable and upright.

The Four Thousand Two Hundred and Fifty Second Year of the Kingdom of Korea, Third Month.

Representatives of the People

A KOREAN APPEAL TO AMERICA
1919

Ahn Ch'ang-ho, who served as chairman of
the Executive Council of the Korean National
Association at the time of the March first
demonstrations, issued this appeal at San
Francisco in order to win American public
opinion over to the side of Korean people.

Source: Ch'ang-ho Ahn, "A Korean Appeal to America," The Nation, Vol.
108, No. 2807, April 19, 1919, pp. 638-639.

We, the representatives of Korea, in this hour of her dire need, issue
to you, our fellow-Christians and citizens of the world's foremost Power,
an appeal for justice and humanity. In great trouble, after prayer to Al-
mighty God, we have turned to you as our only refuge.

For ten years we have been oppressed by a militaristic and imperialis-
tic government. With no more right than Germany when she crushed Belgium under her heel and brought down upon herself the condemnation of
Christendom, the Japanese Government has not only robbed us of national
liberty, but has deprived us of those rights which are the heritage of every
human being. It has deprived us of justice, of freedom of thought, of our
language, of the right to educate our children according to our ideals, im-
posing upon us a system of education not only destructive of our national
ideals, but imperilling the very foundations of the Christian religion.

They have also taken from us the sacred right of religious freedom.
The Christians have been the repeated objects of brutal and nation-wide
persecution and oppression, many having suffered imprisonment and barbarous and inhuman treatment without any just cause.

The story of the numerous outbursts of cruelty, of the wholesale slaugh-
terings, of the systematic oppression which has employed every form of
inhumanity, which has not only robbed our people of their homes but has
made it almost impossible for many to make a living, driving them to des-
peration and starvation, and of the cunning press which kept the truth from
the world by flaunting in its eyes a story of material progress, is a tragic
and pathetic tale which cries out before God and humanity.

At last our race has arisen and proclaimed to the world, in no mistaken
terms, its desire for liberty and for freedom from oppression and unbearable tyranny. No force has been employed. The new movement in Korea
which has attracted the attention of the world is no more than a legitimate
and spontaneous expression of a national conviction.

But the Japanese have replied with force and brutality. The Christian
church in Korea, especially, has become again the center of a barbarous

persecution. Christians have been made to bear crosses in mockery of their religion, while the name of Christ has been subjected to infamy. A little girl who held up the proclamations of independence in her hands had her arms severed. Thousands have been imprisoned and tortured; thousands have been killed. Can the Christian church in America stand passively by without even raising a voice in protest?

The hour for Korea has struck, and the fate of Christ's kingdom in our country hangs in the balance, for even religion cannot withstand this fatal process of denationalization and deracination.

The great war has ushered in a new day for the human race. With ten millions of lives the world has bought freedom from autocracy and militarism. The right of self-determination has been declared universal. The world has been rejoicing over the incoming of a new era when international oppression and of small nationalities are to be protected by a World League of Nations.

To you, citizens of that nation which has been the leader in this epoch-making movement, we appeal. Are the principles of the World's new League mere shibboleths, or are they joyous proclamations of a new day on earth? Do they apply only to Europe, or are they world-wide in their scope? Has the world defeated militarism and imperialism in Germany only to let it stalk its bloody and untrammelled course in the Far East? Surely not. And surely America will not, cannot, stand by and let us suffer. At least the Christian churches of America will lift a voice in protest and in appeal that justice be done, and that those principles for which so many precious American lives were sacrificed shall become the heritage of the world, shall be operative not only in Europe but in the Far East, shall usher in for Korea, too, a new day of justice and freedom from oppression.

DECLARATION OF THE DONGJI-HOI
1921

Syngman Rhee, who became the first president
of the Republic of Korea in 1948, created the
Dongji-hoi, or the Comrade Society in Honolulu,
Hawaii in order to have the society support his
own political activites for Korea's national independence.

Source: Won-yong Kim, Chae-Mi Hanin osimnyonsa, Reedley, California:
Charles Ho Kim, 1959, pp. 199-200.

Factionalism and ill feeling among some Koreans have created a threat
against the Korean Provisional Government-in-exile. There is a need in
the Hawaiian Islands for an organization that will support the Government
loyally and conscientiously and defend the Government against such a threat.
Therefore, we hereby declare the establishment of the Dongji-hoi, or the
Comrade Society and its rules.

Rules

1. The name of the organization shall be called the Dongji-hoi, or
the Comrade Society.
2. The purpose of the Society shall be to protect the Korean Provisional Government-in-exile in Shanghai and to promote unity. The Society
shall protect the Government against any unjust and disloyal persons who
may attempt to interfere with or defame the authority of the Korean Provisional Government-in-exile, and shall deal with such persons with due
measures.
3. The mission of the Society shall be to assist the Chairman in the
execution of his policies and to obey orders without any conditions or hesi-
tations.
4. The headquarters of the Society shall be located in Honolulu and its
branch offices shall be established in various regions.

KOREANS CELEBRATE MARCH 1st
1922

On the third anniversary of the Declaration of
Korean Independence, this speech was delivered
in Korean to a group of Koreans gathered in New
York by a Korean who apologized for his poor
command of his mother tongue.

Source: "Koreans Celebrate March 1st," Korea Review, Vol. IV, No. 2,
1922, pp. 15-16.

This being a purely Korean meeting for the cause of Korea, every one
should speak the Korean language if he can. I must confess my Korean is
not good enough to use in a public address on an occasion like this, but I
am going to try to the best of my ability.

We are all here to celebrate the third anniversary of the Declaration
of Korean Independence from Japan and to commemorate the heroic and
patriotic deeds of those who were the leaders and participants of this wonderful movement which was the first real indication of the renaissance of
the Korean race. If I were an orator or poet, I could translate my thoughts
and sentiments into beautiful language that would stir your patriotic soul
with lofty emotions, but unfortunately not being one, I must content myself
with a few words that will, in a measure, express my thoughts and ideas
concerning our future movements.

Let us consider Korea as our dying mother. Her throat is in the brutal grip of our enemy who is gradually but inexorably strangling her to
death. We, her children, are standing around busying ourselves with tri-
fles and our own petty comforts, letting her die this ignominious death.
Can we honestly consider ourselves her worthy children under the circumstances? No, we must truthfully confess and acknowledge that we are not
doing our sacred duty towards our beloved mother. We ought to be ashamed
to look at the reflection of our faces in the mirror and we ought to consider
ourselves as the most ignoble and the most despicable creatures under the
sun unless we do something to relieve her.

You might say that you want to help her but cannot because you do not
know how. Again, some of you might say that you could help her if you
had soldiers, guns, battleships, airplanes, poisonous gas and other imple-
ments of war. But you find that not only you do not know how to help her,
but also that you have no weapons with which to combat your enemy. So
you consider that you are helpless, and do nothing to prevent your mother's
death. If any of you accept that view of the situation, you are unfit to call
yourself a worthy son or daughter of your mother. I admit that our situation is desperate and our mother's life is in grave danger, but I do not

think it is hopeless unless our people everywhere accept that fatal and pessimistic view. Supposing that it is helpless; we cannot sit idle and wait for our enemy to crush out the last of her flickering life.

I want to make a confession to you, as confession is good for the soul. Three years ago today I entertained the sort of view which I now condemn. If any of you know my personal history of the last thirty-five years, you would not censor me for having had such a view. I thought then that our race was so completely putrefied that it could never be revivified. This view was entertained by the people of other countries and they logically treated Korea in a most shameful and contemptible fashion. As you know, the world does not waste its sympathy or consideration on a hopeless person or hopeless nation. Even now you will find many foreigners who consider us hopeless and continue to accord us the same contemptible treatment as they have heretofore.

But for myself I know our people better than they do, and I fully realize that a great change has taken place in the hearts of the Koreans. This is especially marked among the younger generation in Korea, where they have been suffering so terribly under Japanese oppression. The uprising of 1919 was the first indication of this change for which all ought to be thankful to God, whose power has brought this wonderful hope into their hearts. I believe that the people of Korea have seen the light and they will never go back to the darkness from which they have emerged. Having this belief and cherishing this hope I naturally ask myself: What is my duty now towards our dying mother?

Those of us who are in America or in any other distant country cannot do much in the fundamental change that is going on in the homeland, but we can help her from the outside in this great work of transformation. What are some of the things that we can do from the outside?

(1) To create public sentiment in the world in behalf of our race. The world knows so little of Korea, a very few people really care whether she survives or perishes. We must inform the world concerning us in order that the right treatment will be accorded to us and that it may not believe all the horrible things the Japanese have said about us. To do so a publication is necessary in conjunction with public lectures by competent people who understand us. With that idea uppermost, the "Korea Review" was started three years ago and through this medium we have gained thousands of friends for Korea. If we had the necessary means we could make it larger and more attractive, so that its circulation would be rapidly increased.

I have so far addressed over three hundred different American audiences of various sizes and kinds during the last three years. How many people have heard the story of Korea I am not prepared to say, but it is safe to state that at least 100,000 Americans have heard it. That is not enough; if we have the means we ought to let millions hear it from one end of the country to the other. Of course, one or two persons cannot cover such a large territory with one hundred million people in it. We must have more speakers and we must have more effective organizations for publicity.

(2) One of the most important things that we must do is to educate some of our young men and women in technical schools. There are at least five hundred young people in America and Hawaii who understand English and have sufficient primary education to send to technical institutions to learn science, arts or trades that are absolutely necessary for the well being of the people and the upbuilding of the nation's industry and commerce. We ought to pick out the best material from the Korean communities outside of Korea and help them to learn these vital things. If we educate say one hundred and send them back to Korea every year, they will be a great help to our people at home.

(3) We ought to have combined religious and social centers in every Korean community of any size in America. We ought to have these centers in charge of honest and earnest Christians who will give others religious and social training. That will keep them clean in body and mind and the social intercourse will make them united and friendly, thus eliminating the spirit of factionalism and discord among our people.

(4) We ought to have one good Korean newspaper in America and one in Hawaii. These papers ought to be helped financially from one central source so that their politics will be the same and their work ought to coordinate. There is one paper in San Francisco now and another in Honolulu. They have done very well as far as they can go, but on account of lack of financial support and the system of coordination, their usefulness is diminished. If these papers obtain their support from one united source, and their policies are based upon the principle of cooperation, they will become potent factors in cementing and moulding together all our people as one unit.

(5) If possible, we must encourage some of our people to go into business. We can pick out honest and talented men to buy and sell the merchandise with which they are familiar. We must also encourage some of our people to go into the agricultural industry, especially those who are in the West. By proper methods and supervision these people can be assisted financially so that they can start and carry on these enterprises and not fail in their attempts through the lack of knowledge and sufficient capital.

It is needless for me to tell you that this can never be accomplished unless and until the Korean people everywhere join their hearts and hands in the efforts and they must have a competent general manager whose integrity and ability merit such confidence. Please remember the fact that our enemy is united, therefore he has power and he can do things. You must imitate him in that respect.

I will close by reading you a poem by Oliver Wendell Holmes:

> Build thee more stately mansions, O my soul,
> As the swift seasons roll,
> Leave each new temple nobler than the last,
> Shut thee from heaven with a dome more vast
> Till thou at length art free,
> Leaving thine outgrown shell by Life's unresting Sea.

THE THREE PRINCIPLES OF THE DONGJI-HOI
1924

The Dongji-hoi held a conference in Honolulu on
November 23, 1924 and elected Syngman Rhee its
life-time chairman. It also adopted its Three
Principles, which was printed subsequently in all
of the publications issued by the Dongji-hoi.

Source: Won-yong Kim, Chae-Mi Hanin osimnyonsa, Reedley, California:
Charles Ho Kim, 1959, pp. 203-204.

1. The Three Items of Agreement proclaimed in the Declaration of
Independence shall be observed; let us carry out our great mission in the
spirit of non-violence and self-sacrifice, always demonstrating the spirit
of the March First and asserting justice and humanity.

2. Systematic action is the mother of success; we shall therefore forsake individual acts resolutely, respect order within the organization and
obey the leadership.

3. The economic freedom is the life of a nation; let us promote self-
reliance together.

THE STORY OF KOREAN IMMIGRATION
1932

Lee Tai Sung, executive secretary for the Korean
Student Christian Movement of Hawaii, claimed
that Koreans emigrated to the Hawaiian Islands
in search of wealth and religious freedom.

Source: Tai Sung Lee, "The Story of Korean Immigration," The Korean
Students' of Hawaii Yearbook, 1932, pp. 47-49.

Korea, one of the most ancient of existing nations, has had a very var-
ied and checkered history. Her people have been noted for their stoicism
and timidity rather than for any other qualities that might be said to possess them. At first glance this would seem a combination that would only
make for failure, but the place that Korea has and does hold in the world
proves that for longevity and growth the combination holds good and makes
good.

It seems a far cry from Korean conditions in the last few centuries to
Korean life in Hawaii today. Yet a hasty glance at those conditions will
make more plain the life of Koreans as lived here today. Timidity has always prevented the Korean from antagonizing with force those exigencies
which make for suffering. Rather has she suffered in silence than to make
any material or important attempt along militaristic lines towards allevia-
tion of that suffering. Her very timidity has made her stoic and it has only
been within recent decades that she has made a world-wide ado about things
that she has always borne in silence.

Suffering has been the lot of Korea and Koreans for many ages. Relief
from suffering has been the goal towards which in timidity and stoicism,
they have looked forward for ages. Just what these trials and tribulations
have been, just how these people have been afflicted because of their timidity, is a matter of history and cannot be detailed here. But because of these
conditions, the lot of Korea A.D. 1885 had nearly become unbearable.
Paganism had done its worst. Corrupt government was grinding the life
from the laboring classes. Korea was in the condition that the world was
in at the time of the advent of Christ, sinking in a slough of despondency
that was fast obliterating her personality as a nation.

It was at this critical stage in her history that the great and good missionary, Dr. and Mrs. H.G. Underwood, and Rev. and Mrs. Henry G. Appenzeller, appeared in Korea and began telling the wonderful story of the
Cross and what it could do for those who would accept it and undertake to
carry it through life.

To the timid, stoical Korean, the message was one of hope and life.
Eagerly he asked of its power and a sample of its results. The one was

told him by the missionaries, the other was pointed out to him in the advanced life of the United States. Soon the United States was the hope of Korea, for was it not there that the wondrous Cross had brought beneficent results? Was it not there that the pagan ceased from troubling and the Christian could rest? Was it not worth the while of any timid, down-trodden Korean laborer to make the attempt of reaching this haven of peace and plenty?

REASONS WHY THEY CAME TO HAWAII
As the Korean embraced Christianity, he began to look for a place where it might be lived in peace. So, when in 1903, the call came for him to emigrate to a country where he could enjoy religious freedom and make sugar for wages that, to him, was ideal. The teachings of the missionary had prepared him for emigration, and Koreans to the number of 7,296 landed in Hawaii during the years 1903, 1904 and 1905.

To say that the Christian urge was the greatest among the many that was bringing this strange people from a far-away land to Hawaiian shores, would probably not be true. But it must be counted as one of the forces that caused these timid folks to leave the home which had been theirs for centuries.

It has been mentioned above that wages in Korea were nothing. The laborer was worse off than the beggar. His life was but a mere existence just beyond the pale of starvation. To the laboring class in Korea, the call to work where fuel and shelter were assured, with any kind of a cash wage, was a call to the land of abundance, and he came because of his opportunity to earn what, to him, was a respectable wage.

HOW THEY LIVE IN HAWAII
With the three reasons given above in mind, it will be interesting to note how the Korean population lives in Hawaii.

Perhaps more than any other race, they have lived without conflict save among themselves. Many instances are on record where the Korean camp has been the neutral ground in racial strife. The 7,296 men, women and children that landed here in 1903-1905 now number 6,461. Then, the majority were men in the laboring age of life. Today, the majority are women and children and their relation with the other races is most amicable.

Among the most noteworthy qualities which they possess may be mentioned thrift, industry, and the desire to secure an education and become Americanized. That they are thrifty people is shown by the many successful business men that are doing business in the territory today. While a few of these businessmen arrived here with money in small amounts, the greater number of them have come from the ranks of the laborers and are doing business on capital which they accumulated by the savings of wages. As a proof to their thrift and ability, they point with considerable pride to the fact they hold many of the best-paying positions and that a Korean rarely ever loses a position or resigns save to accept a better one.

Along educationl lines, they have certainly distinguished themselves.

A larger percentage of the Korean population is pursuing higher education than any other race in the territory. It is also true that the percentage of illiteracy is very low among the Koreans. Very early in their history here we find that they established schools for such of their numbers as could not afford to educate themselves.

The majority of them are still engaged in the sugar industry. They have never forgotten that it was to grow sugar that they came to this country, and that it was the sugar industry that paid them the wages that have made them what they are in Hawaii today. Though found in the plantation life of all plantations in the territory, the majority of them are still on Oahu. Every year, sees a Korean drift to Oahu which outnumbers the drift away. About 1,400 of the 6,461 on other Islands are on the plantations, and of this 5,000 are on Oahu.

It is to be deplored that among themselves they are not so amicable. Indeed, they are their own worst enemies. Strife among Koreans has become a proverb, but leaders are looking forward to the near future when inter-Korean quarrels will be no more.

During the recent Pan-Pacific Educational Conference here, the Koreans showed their Pan-Pacific spirit. Their leaders were much in evidence, intelligently so, throughout the entire conference. An investigation made since the conference shows that none of the races received a more intelligent write-up of that conference than did the Koreans and that none of the races were more earnest readers. The entire population was interested in that conference and the interest was of the intelligent, well-informed kind.

HAWAII IS THEIR HOME

The Koreans, through their leaders and their periodicals, are very emphatic in their statements that Hawaii is their home. They point with pride to their children who are becoming American citizens. They tell with even greater pride of the young people who go to the Mainland to secure higher education but almost invariably return here to use that education in the upbuilding of Korean life in Hawaii.

They insist that here they found what has made many of them happy and contented, that here their children are growing up into citizens of whom any nation may be proud. They say, "Here we have lived and here we will die. To us, more than to any other race, is the name 'Paradise of the Pacific' a reality."

THE KOREANS IN HAWAII
1934

Bernice Bong Hee Kim, a graduate of the University
of Hawaii, made a general survey of Koreans in the
Hawaiian Islands in this article.

Source: Bernice Bong Hee Kim, "The Koreans in Hawaii, " Social Science,
Vol. IX, No. 4, October 1934, pp. 409-413.

The Koreans in the Hawaiian Islands, although small numerically,
6, 461 in 1930, only 1. 8 percent of the total population, are a people about
whom one hears peculiar reports. Local newspapers picture political and
nationalistic movements among them, sociologists point out a high frequency
of adult and youthful delinquents, and gossip has it that within that racial
group, all is not well. In business and commercial enterprises, the Koreans do not play a large part. The people have less wealth per capita than
the other Oriental groups. The young Americans of Korean ancestry are
not a homogeneous group, but seem to lean this way and that in an effort to
orient themselves in a new life and a strange environment, and to grope
for leadership in this land where they have learned about the principles of
democracy and untrammelled economic opportunity.

This paper is the result of a study to interpret the Koreans in Hawaii
through their natural environmental and social background and especially
to picture the outlook of yougn Americans of Korean ancestry in the light
of present economic opportunity and their social heritage.

Korea is a peninsula off the northeast coast of Asia, between 34° and
43° north latitude. Its climate is mainly of the modified continental type.
Most of Korea is mountainous and only one-fifth of the total area is cultivated. An uneven coastline fronting the east, south, and west gives Korea
many good harbors and ports so that almost each of the thirteen provinces
has an important seaport.

Koreans claim that their civilization dates from 2333 B. C. with the
coming of Tan Gun, the legendary founder of the Korean nation. Early in
Korean history, with the advent of the Chinese scholar Kija (or Kitze in
Chinese) in 1122 B. C. , the native civilization became greatly influenced
by Chinese civilization and culture. Kija introduced the Chinese system
of writing in Korea, and Chinese literature became the common heritage
of the Koreans. But throughout subsequent similarity in custom and culture,
the two peoples remained as distinct as the French and English. Into the
Korean vernacular were incorporated Chinese words but the groundwork
of the sentence remained essentially Korean. Along with the Chinese literature, came Confucianism, a code of ethics - a social system rather than
a religion. For three thousand years Korea came in close contact with

China but this blending of cultures did not denationalize the Koreans.

There are four main aspects of the cultural background of the Korean: (1) The great respect and almost fetish worship of learning. Korea, like China, early had the civil service examination system to reward properly her deserving scholars. Education became a means to all worthwhile ends. (2) Filial piety and ancestor worship. The foremost duty of every son and daughter was to render complete fealty to parents. (3) The Yangban philosophy. At the top of Korea's social stratification was the Yangban or gentleman class. Its particular virtues were immense pride, dignity, polish, and love of leisure. Practically, the Yangban were of little value because their lives were so unproductive and deadening. Yet to the average Korean, the ideal existence and manner of living were embodied in that group. (4) The subservient position of women. Not only were women subservient to the male members of the family, but their lives were secluded and the higher the social rank, the more complete the seclusion. Men and women were distinctly separated.

Korea was the last of the three oriental nations to open its doors to the Western world. Well-guarded seclusion earned for her the name, The Hermit Kingdom. When the Western world finally forced her out of her isolation during the late 1880's, Korea was found to be in the ancient handicraft stage of economic development --her practices and arts thousands of years old, and in the main, barely altered by the passage of time. The coming in of Christianity, the decadence of the dynastic rule in Korea, and the Japanese filibustering and maneuvers caused general unrest and uncertainty throughout the kingdom. In an amazingly short time the Hermit Kingdom --at the crossroads in the Orient--found itself a bone of contention and a field of battle for China, Russia, and Japan. The people found their ancient complacency and security rudely shaken and reshaken.

It was amidst this turmoil that there came news and encouragement of a better and fuller life away from Korea. During the last six months of 1902 there were announcements made and posters placed at various congregating points in port cities--Chemulpo, Wonsan, Mokpo, Fusan and others --telling about Hawaii and its waving sugar cane fields, and inviting people from the land of the morning calm to share the sunshine of a new land in the middle of the Pacific. At first the fear of the unknown prevented the people from seriously considering leaving home. It was the Christian Koreans who began the emigration movement in the early part of 1903 -- a movement lasting only from 1903 to early 1905.

Within that short period over 7,000 Korean emigrants came to the Hawaiian Islands. Heterogeneity characterized the Korean immigrant group. There were people from every province of Korea, from all walks of life. Very few came from the rural districts, so that the farming class made up less than one-seventh of the entire group. The largest proportion was common laborers or coolies who worked periodically in port cities and towns, next, ex-soldiers of the Korean army (who had sensed Japanese encroachment), then manual laborers, household servants, policemen, wood-

cutters; and miners. Over 6,000 of them were young men between the ages
of twenty and thirty and the remaining few were young married couples.

Each boatload of immigrants was parcelled out to various sugar cane
plantations, so that many friends and relatives were widely separated.
Each plantation had a camp set aside for the Korean laborers and within it
thirty or forty young men and three or four families lived. Korean customs
and modes prevalied in those Korean camps. For example, the few women
there kept very much to themselves. Korean clothes were worn and Korean
fashions persisted. Each camp was like a small unit of the old Hermit Kingdom transplanted to another land.

The general reaction to plantation work and life was one of disappoint-
ment. The carelss, impatient young bachelors were continually in debt
from month end to month end. Within three years about 2,000 Koreans, by
depriving themselves of everything but the barest sustenance, returned to
Korea. About a thousand went to Mainland America to work in the rice
fields in California. Some of them had raised rice in Korea. All of them
had seen it growing and used it as a staple article of food.

For a few years the remaining Koreans in Hawaii moved together in a
general way, with common aims and ambitions. Then in 1910 came news
that Korea was annexed to Japan, rendering these people citizens of neither
here nor there. This event tended to separate the Koreans into two factions.
On one hand, under the leadership of a Korean Ph.D. from Princeton, there
arose a group who dedicated their lives and resources to gaining immediate
independence for Korea. On the other hand, were unimaginative, practical
souls who viewed the situation with less impassioned eyes, and remained
under the wing of an American Methodist organization in an attempt to solve
the immediate problems confronting them. This cleavage has remained
throughout the years and has proven costly in many ways.

Perhaps we can better understand the economic weakness of the Korean
group when we realize that out of the meager pay the laborers received,
they supported educational, religious and political institutions, each of
which demanded its share of money. The above factors, their recent arrival upon the industrial scene, and their small number do not particularly
point to some inherent weakness or deficiency in the Korean make-up.

In Dr. Romanzo Adams' study, The Peoples of Hawaii, he states that
the Korean group at the present time shows a relatively high proportion
living in urban centers. There were two distinct movements toward the
city. From 1910 to 1923 about a thousand bachelors obtained picture brides
from Korea. These prospective grooms all had to come to Honolulu to facilitate arrangements and wait for their brides. They had enticed the mai-
dens in part, with glowing accounts of the plentiful and pleasant life in Hawaii. Many of them, therefore, did not like to take their wives back to the
hard life of the plantation, so they remained about Honolulu and eventually
settled there.

This bringing in of picture brides had several distinct effects. First
of all, it was a source of depletion of finance for the thousand men and per-

haps another thousand friends who assisted financially because, on the
average, it cost a man about $300 to $500 to bring in a wife and establish
a household. Secondly, these picture brides had the good effect of greatly
modifying an ancient North and South sectionalism. Many grooms were
Northerners, and nearly all of the brides were Southerners because that
part of the country was most over-populated and poor. Girls from other
sections of Korea would not come to this strange country to be married to
strange men. Thus at the present time, sectional lines have largely dis-
appeared.

Another impetus to the country-to-city movement was the Japanese
plantation strike in 1919, effective mainly on the Island of Oahu. There
was offered an opportunity to make "good money" by coming to Oahu as
strike-breakers. Many came and few returned to the other islands. Though
the trouble lasted less than a year, those who came were able to save
money and start life in Honolulu, most of them in the Liliha and Palama
districts.

During the first period when men came to Honolulu for their brides,
there was an interim of waiting during which they tried to find some kind
of work. They were able to find employment in the Dole pineapple cannery
and at the docks. The pineapple industry was just beginning its upward
climb and work was to be had by all who applied. Men who worked as ste-
vedores and dockhands were doing what they had done in port cities in Korea. The Liliha district was chosen because it was near the cannery and
waterfront, making it easier and cheaper to travel to and from work. Also,
the rent was very low. Before long there was a community of Koreans.
Some coming later from the other islands sought their friends and settled
in Liliha, others in Palama.

Against the general background and setting of poverty and nationalistic
aspiration, the older generation soon found a barrier of misunderstanding
arise between themselves and the younger generation now growing up. The
following were and still are some of the major points of conflict: (1) Language. The Hawaiian-born Korean can speak English better than Korean
and tends to speak and know less of the ancestral tongue. In some families
parents and children can converse only upon the simplest matters of everyday life. (2) Filial piety. Usually the younger generation does not truly
understand the meaning of filial piety, and the other generation is dogmatic
in its demands and wishes. The ensuing criticisms from the older people
tend to augment the misunderstanding. (3) Social freedom. The average
adolescent boy and girl are left without useful guidance and receive only
adverse criticisms from the older people. The Korean customs of maidenly
modesty and seclusion still forms the unnecessary conflicts and unhappi-
ness than any other single factor.

While the energy and resources of the older folk were consumed by efforts at making a living and agitating for independence for their former
country, their children passed them by and there ensued a conflict between
old Korea and young America. Within a generation, the change from Ko-

rean to American ideas and practices has taken place. The transition has been too rapid and heedless for the preservation of a well-integrated personality. An attempt to incorporate quickly new ideas and practices, no doubt, forms a major factor in the comparatively high proportion of youthful delinquents.

One opportunity unreservedly taken advantage of is that of education. In spite of tremendous handicaps, the Korean students in Hawaii compare favorably with the older, more numerous Oriental groups, both in achievement and proportional representation. Though the Koreans lag behind in other lines, in intellectual progress and in the professions they are rapidly taking prominent places. In the race for economic success, though one shows ability and talent, a Korean boy or girl cannot hope to receive aid from his parents but instead, when he or she begins to earn a living, must take care of them and younger members of the family. Relieved of such a handicap, the future holds greater possibilities for the able young Korean.

At the present time the problem of the younger generation is to preserve personal and racial integrity against the disintegrating forces. Factional division indoctrinated from childhood has tended to divide the young Koreans into groups. There is an urgent need for enlightened leadership, to induce the young people to rise above future for the Korean community as a whole will be especially the guidance of the children of the picture brides. They form the majority of young Koreans of tomorrow. Their fathers will soon be old and will pass away leaving them without paternal aid or guidance while they are yet children or in early adolescence. The mothers, not having had an American education, have little in common with their boys and girls. Upon the successful solution of the problem will depend the future of the young Korean citizens of America in Hawaii.

THE SECOND CONSTITUTION
OF THE KOREAN NATIONAL ASSOCIATION
1937

> The first constitution of the Korean National As-
> sociation was adopted on March 24, 1909. This
> was later replaced by the second constitution,
> which was adopted and put into effect on January
> 1, 1937. The constitution consisted of fifteen
> chapters and fifty-four articles. The following
> is the first chapter of the constitution.

Chapter I

Article 1: The Association shall be composed of the Korean residents
in America, and the name of the Association shall be called the Korean National Association. (The Korean residents in America shall include also
Koreans in Cuba and Mexico.)

Article 2: The purpose of the Association shall be to promote the common well-being of Koreans and to push forward the independence movement
to restore our fatherland, while respecting freedom and equality.

Article 3: The following platform is established to achieve the goals
of the Association:
1. Rendering social services.
2. Promotion of education.
3. Promotion of economic development.
4. Assistance to the Korean Provisional Government-in-exile.
5. Encouragement of the patriotic spirit among Koreans.

Article 4: The Association shall establish two divisions; the headquarters shall consist of Plenary Conference of the Delegates, Central Executive Committee, Central Standing Committee and Central Supervisory Committee, while the regional branch shall consist of Regional Conference, Regional Executive Committee, Regional Standing Committee and Regional
Supervisory Committee.

Article 5: The Central Headquarters of the Association shall be established in Los Angeles, California, United States of America.

THE RULES OF HUNGSA-DAN
1947

The original rules of the Hungsan-dan, or the
Corps for the Advancement of Individuals went
into effect when the corps was established on
May 13, 1913. The following is from the revised rules, which went into effect in 1947.

Source: Won-yong Kim, Chae-Mi Hanin osimnyonsa, Reedley, California:
Charles Ho Kim, 1959, pp. 177-178.

Article 1. The Corps shall be called the Hungsa-dan, or the Corps
for the Advancement of Individuals.

Article 2. The Corps shall protect and secure righteousness by uniting
loyal men and women who consider truth-seeking and labor as their life,
shall develop good character by uniting and cultivating virtue, knowledge
and sound body, and shall lay foundations for the prosperity of our people
by developing the sacred organization.

Article 3. In order to achieve the purpose of the Corps the following
training shall be carried out:
1. Training shall be conducted to help cultivate virtuous character in
the spirit of truth-seeking, labor, loyalty and courage, to develop strength
by disciplining body, and to develop healthy character by learning special
knowledge or vocational skills.
2. Training shall be conducted to help secure trust, to help obey rules,
to help assist in time of need, and to help develop the sacred organization.
3. Training shall be conducted to help develop an independent spirit
and the ability for self-government, to help cultivate social awareness and
public spirit and to help enhance the national character.
4. In order to advance the purpose of the Corps various mass movements necessary for the revolution of the national character and for the
strengthening of people will be carried out by the members of the Corps.
The Corps shall also provide its members with experiences in social services.
5. In accordance with the necessity of carrying out practical works
the Corps shall operate cultural organizations, shall provide social services, and shall establish model villages and vocational schools.
6. In view of the permanent nature of the Corps, it shall not engage
in political activities. (However, individual members shall have the right
to participate in political activities as an individual according to his conscience and belief.)

7. In order to remind always the Corps members of the resolution, the following pledge shall be used as a guide for everyday life:

a. Let us dedicate ourselves endlessly in the spirit of righteousness, labor, loyalty and courage.

b. Let us love each other, let us defend our belief and righteousness, and let us help each other in adversity.

c. Let us obey and sacrifice together for the sake of the Corps.

d. Let us keep honesty in all matters, and let us discharge our responsibility that is given to us.

e. Let us forsake our individual interests and dedicate ourselves to our nation and people.

A KOREAN IMMIGRANT
1949

Morris Pang's father, one of the Korean emigrants who came to the Hawaiian Islands as
laborers between 1903 and 1905, told his life
story to Morris when he was asked by his son.

Source: Morris Pang, "A Korean Immigrant," Social Forces in Hawaii,
XII, 1949, pp. 19-24.

"Hello, Aboji (father). How are you feeling tonight?"

"I am fine, son. What brings you here by my home on such a rainy night?"

"Ive heard you tell interesting episodes of your experiences in Korea, China,
Russia, Japan, and on a plantation in Hawaii, and I wondered if you would
combine these stories together and tell me the story of your life."

Outside the raid fell in a steady downpour, sometimes increasing in
intensity, sometimes decreasing, and then stopping for a little while only
to start again. But we were all snug and warm inside and for the next two
hours, I sat in the parlor with Aboji while he told me his life history.

"I was born in Hangkyung-do, Kilju, Korea, in 1878," he began. "I
was the ninth child in a family of ten children. In comparison with our
neighbors, our family was well off, for although we had no money as such,
we had land, houses, cows, pigs, and chickens. You see, the possession
of such goods was considered to be restricted to the wealthy. Thus, I say
that we were quite well to do. Indeed we had much wealth then, especially
with all the grain that we had. I can remember still how we worked in the
fields all summer and then harvested the grain in such quantities that the
pile would grow higher and higher, and wider and wider around the base.
No, we didn't have money but we were well off.
"Many of our neighbors were not as fortunate as we were, however,
and they were forced to send their sons to Russia or to Manchuria to work.
Sometimes whole families went to Manchuria to live. Some of them came
back and told us wonderful tales of the countries outside our village.
"Because my family could afford it, I was sent to school instead of
working in the fields. I remained in school until the sixth grade. Then
one night, twenty-five of us stole away from home to seek our fortunes in
Russia and to see some of the wonderful things we had heard so much about.
"We stayed in Russia for about fourteen years, working as laborers
at first, and as contract laborers later. We were engaged in all kinds of

work--sometimes in building roads, and sometimes in building railroads.
While doing the latter type of work in Vladivostok in 1902 and 1903, the Japanese and the Russians went to war. Many people died. We had to leave
or take the chance of being killed. Confusion was everywhere, everybody
was in panic, all the roads and railroads were blocked, and there was no
place to go. We left all we had earned and fled for our lives. Many mer-
chants and businessmen who stayed back to try to sell their property lost
their lives because of their delay. We couldn't go back to Korea because
the roads were blocked. Finally, we were able to get passage on an English
ship and sailed for Japan. We were safe on the ship, for the Russians and
the Japanese did not dare fire upon it because of the English flag.

"We stayed in Japan for three months and then were able to get passage
to Korea. When we arrived in Korea, we had no money left, and found that
there were no opportunities for work of any kind and that conditions were
bad. It was then that we heard of a man who was talking a lot about the opportunities in Hawaii. He said that it was a land of opportunity where everybody was rich. He promised to give us work, free houses, and adequate
pay. It all looked very lucrative and so after reading the contract, which
seemed quite suitable, thirteen of us signed. We were shipped to Mountain
View, Hawaii.

"It was not long before we were in the cane fields and cutting away at
the cane stalks. We worked in the hot sun for ten hours a day, and the pay
was fifty-nine cents a day. I was not used to this kind of work and I had a
difficult time. This type of work was indeed harder than the type of contract work that I did in Russia. However, I did the best I could and strug-
gled along with the rest of men.

"Then one day I heard of a Russian physician who lived in the vicinity
of the plantation and who needed an interpreter. I could speak Russian,
Japanese, and Chinese, as well as Korean, so I went to talk to him. At
that time language differences were a serious handicap in inter-racial relations. The physician could speak only English besides his native Russian,
so I interpreted Japanese, Chinese, and Korean for him. The result was
that after about three days in the fields, I became an interpreter.

"After a very short period, however, the physician moved away so that
I had to go back to the plantation. Fortunately, because of my experience
in handling men in Russia and because I had had some schooling and could
read and write well, I soon became one of the lunas (foremen).

"Oh, I had one more experience as an interpreter--with the police department in Hilo. It was at the time of the Russian immigration to Hawaii.
On one occasion the police station had become crowded with Russians and
no one could speak to them. The Korean Interpreter told the sheriff about
me. I did not like the idea, because after the trial there might be hard
feelings. However, the plantation boss told me to go. I went reluctantly.
In the court room, I talked to the Russians and then interpreted what I found
out to the Korean interpreter, who in turn interpreted into English from
my Korean.

"Plantation camp life in those days was greatly different from the type of life we lead now in Hawaii. During those early days on the plantation, we all lived in one big camp. The men were given small houses for themselves and the single men lived in big barracks consisting of one big square sleeping room in which there was no privacy. The men were segregated racially--the Japanese occupying one building, the Chinese another, etc. However, everybody ate in the same place--in a big kitchen. Those who wanted to could cook their own meals, and frequently, some of the men would form a group to cook their own 'racial foods.' Everything in the camp was free except the food. The men who ate in the big kitchen paid six dollars and fifty cents a month. Food was very cheap then, one bag of rice costing only a dollar and fifty cents.

"A working day on the plantation followed the same pattern, day in and day out. The cook would get up at three o'clock in the morning and prepare breakfast and make lunches for the men, who got up at five o'clock. A train would take them to the place of work in the fields, after the lunas had gone to the boss in charge to get their assignments for the day.

"I was in charge of two hundred and fifty workers--two hundred men and fifty women. After receiving my assignment I would take my group out to the fields and begin work at six o'clock. We worked ten hours in the blazing sun and had only a half hour for lunch. As a luna, I was responsible for my group. We worked on a contract basis because it paid more. Some of the plantations paid by the month--eighteen dollars a month. When we contracted, we would get as much as one dollar and twenty-five cents a day. My workers received between seventy-five cents to a dollar and twenty-five cents a day. The women's wages ranged from seventy-five cents to a dollar. As a luna, I was paid seventy-five dollars a month.

"When we got to the fields, I would line the workers up, with the fastest worker at the head of the line, and so on. By doing this, I got more work out of them. A good luna is always kind to his men. If he is mad all the time the men will resent it and work poorly. I had workers of all races in my group--Hawaiians, Filipinos, Puerto Ricans, Chinese, Japanese, Portugese, and Koreans. Every day, the Number Three Boss would inspect the camp after we left for the fields and then would come out to see how we worked. At four thirty o'clock we would quit work and walk wearily back to the train and start for the camp. On the way back, I had to record the men's time. I could tell who they were by their faces, for I knew them well. When we got back to the camp, we ate, washed, and then went directly to bed.

"During the harvesting season, we even worked on Sundays and holidays --seven days a week, ten hours a day. Otherwise we had Sunday off. Some of us went visiting while others just slept.

"There were three Haole bosses. They were good men. They gave us free houses and anything we needed if we were good and did not cause trouble. They did not bother us at all and most of the men liked the bosses. They all lived in big houses quite a distance away."

Thus ended Aboji's long story about his early experiences. The rest of his story was more familiar to me: his marriage, my parents' move to Oahu in 1922, and Aboji's purchase of a laundry there, the growth of the family, sons, daughters, and grandchildren.

As an afterthought I asked Aboji whether he never thought of returning to Korea some day. He replied, "At one time I wanted very much to go back to Korea, but now that I am old and I haven't seen my parents since I was eleven years old, my feelings have changed. I don't even know whether they are alive or not. Besides, I have been in Hawaii a long time and I have a family of my own here. No, I don't care very much to go back to Korea. I am too old. I think I would like to spend the rest of my life in Hawaii."

I thanked Aboji for the story of his life. Seeing that the rain had stopped, and that it was getting rather late, I made ready to leave for my home. As I was leaving the house, I saw Aboji staring into space--probably reminiscing. I wondered what thoughts were running through his head. Perhaps he was recalling the days spent in Hangkyung-do, or Vladivostok, or the ten years on the plantation here in Hawaii.

THE LIVES OF KOREAN WOMEN IN AMERICA
1973

> Ms. Kim, whose first name is not known, pointed
> out the problems of the first-generation Korean
> women in America. A comparison between Ko-
> rean women in Korea and their counterparts in
> America was also made.

Source: Ms. Kim, "The Lives of Korean Women in America," Insight,
Vol. 2, No. 1, January-February 1973, p. 3.

In the thrust of the current women's liberation movement, it is timely
befitting to shed a perspective light on the lives of Korean women here in
the U.S.A. Contrary to the often encountered interpretations that the aim
of the feminist movement is for women to assume the "roles of men," or to
acquire "masculine personalities," or to pursue "masculine goals, achieve-
ments, and fulfillments," and so forth ad infinitum, the foremost goal of
the women's movement is to disseminate a sense of self-awareness, self-
respect, and insight of the position of women as women in whatever social
roles, responsibilities, and commitments she may be engaged in. First,
it is imperative for us women to journey through the process of self-know-
ing and self-examination before we can expect the men to achieve that level
of understanding of us, and vice versa. The many misconceptions about
the movement is often perpetuated by the opposers by way of off-tracked
judgements and distorted broadcasting of the ideas behind the women's
movement. This article is written with the aim in mind of first becoming
cognizant of the situations unique in Korean women's lives.
After the initial step of transplanting one's family into a foreign culture
and nation, there are many obstacles that the family as a whole and as individual members must hurdle through one by one. In my own experience,
I've known some families who manage to hurdle over them very gracefully;
on the other hand there are some families that become terribly bruised during the course. And not all the obstacles are shared by everyone in the
family. For example, there are those problems that are particularly crucial for the children such as that of self-identity within the background of
two very different cultures. Then there are other obstacles such as language problems which are especially difficult for the mother, father, grandparents, and older siblings. Women, particularly mothers and unworking
girls, have suffered the language barrier more acutely than anyone else because of their severely limited contact outside of the home in the American
society. Men, working women, and students have a great deal of social and
intellectual stimulations which enrich their daily experience of not only the
English language but also of the American system of social relationships

and attitudes. And for the older folks, it becomes increasingly difficult because after a certain age, one becomes much less adept at learning a new language and a new way of life. There are many Korean mothers and girls who have lived in the U.S. for several years and not yet have achieved the full fluency which many of us in the younger generation and of course of the second and third generation enjoy without retrospection.

The next major problem is that of social assimilation and acceptance. The process of acculturation is almost invariably smoothest for the children. For the father, it is often a matter of economic survival, therefore he must try to fit into a safe niche. For the mother, it is very difficult to find a comfortable and freely accepting environment in which to fulfill her own needs as a woman mainly because most of her time is spent in the house. This is not to give a pejorative regard to home duties; quite the contrary, it is to recognize that the Korean woman is very dedicated to her home and family. And it is this same solid devotion from which arises the sacrifices of other personal and social fulfillments which she may have aspired at some point in her life.

In general, it is true that the Korean church is the center of social gatherings and activities. For many Korean women, the church is the only source of meeting other Koreans. The students have the school social life, the fathers have the job life, and so do the other Koreans who work. This problem may not be appreciated by all Koreans because many of them live in regions such as New York, Los Angeles, Honolulu, Chicago, Washington, etc., where there are oriental communities already established. As recent as 10-15 years ago in some of these same areas, there were only a handful of Korean emigrants. During those years, it was a happy surprise indeed to discover a fellow Korean. At that time, the emigrated Koreans were mostly of professional fields. Now the Koreans who are settling in the U.S.A. are of various classes and backgrounds.

In comparison to the Korean women here in America, the Korean women living in Korea generally have considerably more time due to the domestic help available. Most Korean families there, with the exception of very poor families, have at least one maid (who is often a young girl of 14 or 15 years of age or even younger; and it is becoming very hard to find housekeepers for hire these days in Korea) to help with the cooking, cleaning, washing, grocerying, babysitting, etc. Here in the U.S.A., it is too expensive for most families to hire a housekeeper to do all that work. One might say that due to automation, these household chores should not take so much time. To a certain extent, the various household appliances do provide convenient help, but the fact remains that the Korean woman upon arriving in the U.S. has to assume all these home and child-care duties by herself alone, which can be vast loads of responsibilities especially if the family is large. Many Korean women in Korea carry the misconception that the women in America live in "worldly heaven." To be sure, it is good for the wife to be out of the house of the in-laws and no longer to be a subject of their domination and control, and assert her freedom as a woman as well as a wife and as a mother. However, those Korean women in Korea with their somewhat distorted idea of American living are surprised when told that there is a great deal of hardship that the Korean women go through here in this country.

With the free time that the women in Korea do have, they have the opportunity to become involved in community activities more. Her life in the U.S.A. often does not allot her the time enabling her to become a more socially active member of her neighborhood community. All of these factors --overburdened home duties, family responsibilities such as rearing children in a culturally conflicting setting, the problem of language barrier in relation to both the society and to her children, and so forth all contribute to dampen the full potential of the Korean woman's daily life.

Just as there is a conspicuous difference of past experiences, behaviors, and attitudes between the women from Korean and the Korean-American women born or raised here, there is also a difference between the older and younger Korean-American women of the same generation here in the U.S., just as there would be also in the Korean society. Furthermore, there is also a noticeable difference between the first and second generation, and between the second and third generation Korean-Americans.

Despite these transitioning modes of attitudes and life styles, all Koreans share the common feeling for their native home land, whether it be South Korea or North Korea. The Koreans who have left Korea at some point in their lifetime to start a new life in another country all have the nostalgic longing for their old friends and relatives. The younger members of these families feel a strong urge to regrasp their old roots back in Korea. And as for the second and third generation Koreans, they too are deeply concerned and curious to learn of the land of their parents and grandparents. In any case, we all must try to stretch our experiential capabilities and encompass the past history of our people into an integral part of our understanding of ourselves as Korean-Americans.

HISTORY AND ROLE OF THE CHURCH IN
THE KOREAN AMERICAN COMMUNITY

Source: This was written by the editor for inclusion in this compilation.

When the first large group of Korean immigrants arrived in
Honolulu, Hawaii on January 13, 1903, there were among them some
people who had already embraced Christianity as their religion.[1] These
Christians became active catalysts to the establishment of churches in
the Korean American community in the Hawaiian Islands and the Mainland of the United States. That there were people converted to Christianity among the first group of emigrants from Korea was certainly
not an historical accident; it was closely related to the history of
evangelism in Korean and the cause of Korean emigration to the Hawaiian
Islands.

As early as 1784, Christianity came to Korea in the form of
Catholicism, when Yi Seung-hun, the son of an ambassador to China,
returned to Korea with books, crosses and other Christian artifacts.
He had gone to China to study and was baptized in Peking. In 1794 a
Chinese priest came into Korea crossing the Yalu River border in
secrecy in response to Yi Seung-hun's plea for more priests.

Catholicism began to gain its converts shortly after its arrival
in Korea. Many people dissatisfied with their lot in the present life
turned to the teachings of Catholicism as it promised a better life in the
next world, no matter how vaguely they understood the real meaning of
life after death. Others embraced the religion as it symbolized the
Western scientific knowledge. At any rate, as many Koreans turned to
Catholicism, the Yi court (1392-1910) became deeply concerned with the
doctrine of the Catholic church that preached equality of men and the
brotherhood of mankind. The doctrine was considered dangerous to the
preservation of the Confucian system of loyalties and ancestor worship,
which was the foundation of the kingdom. Therefore, the Yi court issued
an edict in 1785 banning Christianity. Shortly after the ban, many Korean
Christians along with the Chinese priest were put to death and the
persecution of Christians continued. In 1839 three French missionaries
and their Korean followers were executed, and this incident angered
the French government, which sent a ship to Korea in 1846 to demand
an explanation. As late as 1866 three bishops, seventeen priests, and
numerous Korean Christians suffered the Christian martyrdom.

The treaty of 1882 between Korea and the United States and other
treaties the Yi court had been compelled to conclude with other Western
nations brought more Western missionaries to Korea. Although most of
them sought first the wealth of the earthly kingdom upon their arrival
in Korea, a few were dedicated to the cause of the heavenly kingdom. [2]
Among them was Horace N. Allen who was sent to Korea in 1884 by the
Presbyterian Board of Foreign Missions of the United States of America.

Shortly after his arrival in Seoul, an incident occurred that helped him gain the confidence of the king of Korea. During a coup d'etat involving the conservatives and progressives of the Yi court, the queen's nephew was seriously wounded and the missionary doctor was called upon to give him immediate medical attention.[3] His successful treatment of the queen's nephew won him the position of the king's personal physician and the king's approval of Christianity.

For a number of reasons more Koreans in the north accepted Christianity than their countrymen in the south. First of all, Koreans in the northern provinces had been discriminated against by the Yi court which was constantly plagued by regional factionalism. The Yi court sent to the northern provinces government officials who were considered dangerous to the security of the court. It also denied the people from the northern provinces access to high positions in the central government. Such a policy of discrimination pursued by the Yi court eventually led the people to revolt against the central government in an insurrection of 1811 led by Hong Kyong-nae. The rebellion was strongly supported by the people in the north who were also suffering then from a severe famine. Secondly, the North Koreans developed less rigid and more mobile social structure during the Yi Dynasty, due to the lack of arable and in the north, than their countrymen in the south. The North Koreans were therefore exposed to more egalitarian values that made them more amenable to the acceptance of Christian doctrine.

Thirdly, several decisive battles were fought in the northwestern region of Korea, particularly in the vicinity of P'yongyang, the present capital of the Democratic People's Republic of Korea, during the Sino-Japanese War of 1894-95. Koreans became victims between the retreating Chinese soldiers and the advancing Japanese army and much of their property was destroyed in the war, the outcome of which was to determine the political fate of the Korean people in the years to come. Several missionaries stationed in the vicinity of P'yongyang gave their time and effort to alleviate the sufferings of the people caught innocently in a war created by foreign powers. Such an unselfish devotion of missionaries to the care and cure of Koreans afflicted by was gradually endeared them to the Korean people who flocked to churches to learn a better world to live in both spiritually and materially.

American missionaries encouraged by deed or word Koreans to emigrate to the Hawaiian Islands as they saw "an opportunity for Koreans to improve their condition and to acquire useful knowledge and to better themselves financially...," as pointed out by David W. Deshler in his letter to Mr. Huntington Wilson, a charge d'Affaires of the American Legation in Tokyo, who was asked by Deshler to intervene on his behalf after the Korean emigration had been terminated by the Korean government in 1905.[4]

Commenting on the influence of American missionaries on Koreans who made the decision to emigrate to the Hawaiian Islands, Tai Sung Lee, executive secretary for the Korean Student Christian Movement of Hawaii once stated:

It was at this critical stage in her history that the great and good missionary, Dr. and Mrs. H.G. Underwood, and Reverend and Mrs.

Henry G. Appenzeller, appeared in Korea and began telling the wonderful story of the Cross and what it could do for those who will accept it and undertake to carry it through life. To the timid, stoical Korean the message was one of hope and life. Eagerly he asked of its power and a sample of its results. The one was told him by the missionaries, the other was pointed out to him in the advanced life of the United States. Soon the United States was the hope of Korea, for was it not there that the wondrous Cross had brought beneficient results? Was it not worth the while of any timid, downtrodden Korean laborer to make the attempt of re- reaching this haven of peace and plenty? As the Korean embraced Christianity he began to look for a place where it might be lived in peace. [5]

Missionaries were not the only reason for Korean emigration to the Hawaiian Islands. There was a widespread famine in the winter of 1901 in the northwestern region of Korea, and the government made ef- forts to relieve the people from starvation by allowing them to emigrate. Also there were agents from several overseas development companies who were sent to Korea to recruit laborers to work in Hawaiian sugar plantations. One of them was David W. Deshler of the East-West De- velopment Company, who was responsible for the emigration of the first group of Koreans to Hawaii in 1903. [6]

Of all American missionaries, the Reverend George Heber Jones of the Methodist Mission was most influential on Korean emigrants. He came to Korea in 1887 and was later sent to Chemulp'o in 1892 to suc- ceed the Reverend Appenzeller. Chemulp'o, now Inch'on was a port city where Deshler was stationed to recruit Korean laborers. Partly due to his geographical location and partly due to his compassion for Koreans leaving their homeland for a strange place, Jones felt the need to en- courage them by telling them about life in Hawaii. He also gave some leaders among them letters of introduction to the superintendent of the Methodist Mission in Hawaii so that they would be greeted by some- one upon their arrival in Honolulu. The Reverend John W. Wadman, superintendent of the Hawaiian Mission of the Methodist Episcopal church, in his report, "Educational Work Among Koreans," described the role Jones had played in the immigration of Koreans in Hawaii.

While encamped at the seaport of Chemulp'o, awaiting the trans- port to bear them away into a strange land, Reverend George Heber Jones, a Methodist Episcopal Missionary, became interested in their welfare, and held large tent meetings in order to inspire them with laudable ambitions and prepare them for the strange experi- ences so soon to overtake them... He also handed a few of the lead- ers among them letters of introduction to the Superintendent of Methodist Missions in Hawaii, and gave them in parting his heart- felt blessing. [7]

Later in 1906 when Jones published an article "The Koreans in Hawaii," in the Korea Review, the missionary mentioned that he met a Korean and his family whom he had baptized in Korea. [8]

As has been pointed out, some Korean emigrants were converted into Christianity even prior to their departure for the Hawaiian Islands.

Therefore, the history of the church in the Korean American community may be considered a continuing saga of Korean Christianity.

The history of the church in the Korean American community may be divided into four major periods; (1) the period of beginning and growth, 1903-1918, (2) the period of conflicts and divisions, 1919-1945, (3) the period of status quo, 1946-1967, and (4) the period of revival, 1968-1974.

The period between 1903 and 1918 saw a rapid growth in the number of Koreans professing Christianity as their religion. It was estimated that during the period approximately 2,800 Koreans were converted to Christianity and 39 churches were established in the Hawaiian Islands alone. This numerical growth is a remarkable achievement in view of the fact that the total number of persons of Korean ancestry in the Islands during this period was less than 8,000. A number of factors seemed to have contributed to such a phenomenal growth. First, Korean society in the Hawaiian Islands lacked strong social groups established on the basis of traditional ties. Although there were social groups such as clan associations and organizations by sworn brotherhood,[9] they were proven ineffective in dealing with the white Americans. Second, Christianity may have been used as a means of gaining a sympathy from the white Americans. This particular point was alluded to by Jones when he stated:

> One third of all the Koreans in Hawaii are professing Christians. They dominate the life in the camps on the Islands of Oahu, Kauai and Maui where they are stamping out gambling and intoxication. The Koreans have fallen into sympathetic hands in Hawaii.[10]

Third, to those who were not members of either a clan association or sworn brotherhood organization, the church was the only social group that enabled them to engage in social intercourse outside their work camps. Fourth, there seemed to have been a certain degree of group pressure on non-Christians, particularly after a significant number of Koreans had become converts. Thus parents who were not Christians would send their children to church.

During this period several churches of different denominations were established in the Islands and the Mainland of the United States. The first group to establish a church was the Korean Christians of Methodist persuasion. It was on November 3, 1903 that efforts were made to establish a congregation, when a group of Koreans in Honolulu chose Ahn Chung-su and Woo Byong-kil as their representatives to negotiate for a place of worship with a superintendent of the Methodist Mission. As a result, the Korean Evangelical Society was organized a week later and church services were held at a rented house. The society did not receive regular church status until April, 1905 when John W. Wadman was appointed superintendent of the Hawaiian Mission of the Methodist Episcopal church by Bishop John W. Hamilton.[11] Wadman contributed greatly to the growth of the Methodist church in the Korean community in the Hawaiian Islands from the time of his appointment until his resignation on January 1, 1914.[12] He was instrumental in purchasing a piece of property situated on the corner of Punchbowl and Beretania Streets, Honolulu at a sum of $12,000 with the purpose of organizing a boarding school for Korean boys. While serving as super-intendent of the Mission, he also supervised the boarding school, which was then directed by his wife, until June 1913, when Syngman Rhee, the first president of the Republic of Korea, was appointed principal of the school.

It is alleged by Warren Kim, the author of the <u>Chaemi Hanin osimnyon sa</u> (A History of Fifty Years of Koreans in America), that Rhee was given this position by Wadman as an expression of his grati-tude to Rhee, who had helped him settle a dispute between Wadman and the people of the Korean community in the Islands. The dispute began with a local newspaper report on October 5, 1912. In the report it was said that Wadman had received a sum of $750 from a certain Japanese consul of Honolulu who had donated the money with an ostensible purpose of helping poor Koreans. When he was confronted by a group of angry Koreans who hated anything symbolic of Japanese, he acknowledged the receipt of money, although he presented a reason different from the one reported in the newspaper. He said that he had accepted money in order to use it as a part of maintenance expense for the boarding school. Koreans felt it their moral duty to oppose the acceptance of such a financial assistance from an official of the government that had deprived them of their nation in 1910. Wadman was cornered further into an em-barrassing situation as Korean students refused to attend school. At this time Syngman Rhee arrived in Honolulu under the invitation of the Korean National Association. When he was asked by Wadman to intervene in the dispute, he gladly accepted the request and worked toward a solution. With the assistance from Rhee, Wadman managed to avoid a confrontation of a more serious nature, but he also sowed the seed of conflict and dissension by appointing Rhee as principal of the boarding school. [13]

The second Methodist church grew out of the Korean Evangelical Society, which was organized by a group of Korean residents in San Francisco on October 8, 1905. Mun Kyong-ho assumed the responsi-bility of conducting church services until July 15, 1906 when Bang Wha-jung succeeded him as evangelist for the group. The society was ex-panded after Yang Ju-sam arrived in San Francisco on his way to Nash-ville, Tennessee where he was to attend the Divinity School, Vanderbilt University. Upon his arrival he saw everywhere around him the life of adversity and poverty to which his countrymen were subjected. He was so moved emotionally by what he had seen that he decided to post-pone his study in order to take on the work of helping his countrymen spiritually and materially. The society rented a building on California Street and held a church service dedicating the house of worship. The building had three floors. The first floor was used as dining hall for Korean boarders who were accommodated on the third floor. The second floor was used as a place of church services. The society was granted its present church status after the Reverend Yi Dae-wi was appointed as its pastor on August 5, 1911. The congregation moved to the present church building located at Powell Street in June 1928. Today, the Korean Methodist Church of San Francisco, as the oldest Korean church in the Mainland of the United States, has a membership of three hundred dedicated people. Its annual budget as of April 1974 is approximately 21,000 dollars and its total assets are estimated at half a million dollars.[14]

During the first period an Episcopal church was organized in Honolulu by efforts of Chong Hyong-gu and Kim Ik-song who was also known as Isaiah Kim. On February 10, 1905 a church service dedicating the Korean Episcopal Church was held at the St. Andrew Episcopal Church in Honolulu, and the church then rented a classroom at a local elementary school as a place of church services. On October 16 of the same year the church was permitted the use of a part of the St. Elizabeth Episcopal Church, a local Chinese church.

The first period also saw the establishment of a Presbyterian church in Los Angeles, California in 1906, the first Presbyterian church ever to be established in the United States by Korean Christians. A group of Korean residents in Los Angeles sent its representative to negotiate with the Presbyterian Missionary Extension Board for a place of worship. The board responded by dispatching the Reverend Richard who became instrumental in establishing the Korean Presbyterian Mission. The group rented a house situated on Bunker Hill Street as a place of church services. The group did not receive its church status until April 1921.

The second period in the history of the church in the Korean American community was marked with disputes over policy on church administration, church financial business, and operation of the Korean boarding school which was later known as the Choong-ang hakwon, or the Central Institute. As has been noted already, Syngman Rhee was able to secure principalship of the Central Institute in 1913. No sooner he became principal than he wanted to have a lot on the corner of Emma and Punchbowl Streets, which was purchased by the Korean National Association of Hawaii at $1,500. Rhee wanted to use it for a dormitory to accommodate students at the Central Institute. His request was, however, denied by the delegates to the annual convention of the Korean National Association in 1915. Rhee then decided to use a less legitimate but a more effective means of threat and coercion to take the property away from the association. Rhee learned that there had been some irregularities in the business of running the association. It had been said that Hong In-p'yo, treasurer of the association, and Kim Chong-hak, its president, dipped into the public till entrusted to them. Upon learning the irregularities, Rhee demanded that he be given the power to supervise the treasury of the association and that the controversial property be turned over to him for use of the Korean school. Rhee seemed to have orchestrated his demand with another high-handed method. A group of students from the Central Institute led by Yang Yu-ch'an came to the annual convention of the Korean National Association in May 1915 to beat up Yi Hong-ki, Kim Kyu-sop, Yi Chong-kun, and Kim Chong-hak for opposing Rhee's request.[15] The Honolulu Advertiser ran an article concerning this incident in July 1915 under the title, "Korean Trouble Gets Into Court," as follows:

> ...Ahn Heung Kyong, General Manager, charged Hong In Pio for embezzling $120 from membership fees, and Kim Chong Hak for embezzling $1,300. Yi Hong Ki, who was maltreated a month

ago by a mob at Korean National Association brought a trial of 19 men in court... [16]

The beating incident and the revelation of embezzlement of public funds by officers of the association changed the mood of most members of the association. When the request was put again for reconsideration, the delegates reversed their previous decision and thirty-five out of thirty-eight voted for the free grant of the land.

Rhee was not only a catalyst to disputes among Koreans, but also a sharp wedge between the Hawaiian Methodist Mission and some Korean Methodist Christians. When William H. Fry was appointed to succeed Wadman as superintendent on January 1, 1914, he learned that the church financial matters had been dealt with in less than a businesslike manner. He wanted to correct past mistakes in the mission administration by means of his close personal supervision on both the church and the school. Also, it was alleged that Fry was opposed to the use of the church and the school as training centers of political leaders and political activities for the Korean independence movement against the Japanese Empire. Rhee, on the other hand, wanted to use them to teach Korean nationalism and to train Korean political leaders. Furthermore, Rhee refused to take orders from Fry, and challenged him to turn the governance of the school and the church over to Koreans. Rhee was of the opinion that Koreans should have a complete control over the church and the school as they were fully supported by Koreans in the Islands. Such two diametrically opposed positions were certainly destined to travel a separate course sooner or later. [17]

The inevitable separation came in the fall of 1916 when a group of seventy or eighty people left their Methodist church in order to follow Rhee's leadership for the autonomy and self-determination of the church in Korean community. The first church service was held at the residence of Park Nae-soon after their separation, and the separatists then decided to hold their church services at the Korean Girls' Seminary building. In 1917 the place of worship was moved to the school building located at Wailaie Street and 7th Avenue. At the beginning, the congregation was known simply as the Silip kyohoi, or the New Church, which was changed to the Korean Christian Church sometime in 1917. This was not the only New church in the Islands. There was a New church established at Koloa, Kauai as early as 1915, and there was as many as fifteen when the separatist movement reached its zenith.

An important event in the development of New churches took place on December 13, 1918 when the first annual delegates' conference of the Korean Christian churches was held to establish an organization to coordinate various church activities and to discuss methods of combating the established Methodist church. Out of this conference emerged the Korean Christian Missions known as the Central Korean Christian church. The delegates seemed to have agreed on a major weapon to be used in competing with the well established Methodist church supported by a strong missionary organization. The idea of independence and self-government was to be their effective weapon, which was also that of Rhee, who later expressed his philosophy for founding the church in in a letter dated December 12, 1944 to Kingsley K. Lyu:

...When I founded the Korean Christian Church with you people, I was sure I would lose my Korean and American friends in the Methodist Church. But I was resolved that we Koreans should control our own church administration without depending upon the foreign missions; that we should govern our own affairs. It was natural that the Methodists criticized our Christian people and were bitter to us... [18]

From the beginning of the separatist movement to August 1945 when Korea was freed from the Japanese colonialism, the members of the Korean Christian church were an indispensable part of the Korean national independence movement abroad. Ideologically, they advocated as strongly as they could that Koreans were ready to exercise self-government and independence. As evidence they pointed to their Korean church as a symbol of independence from foreign domination and of self-government in admistration of their own affairs. Financially, they sent in their contributions out of their meager earnings as workers on sugar plantations or as manual laborers.

The rapid growth of the Korean Christian churches in the islands seemed to have had an adverse effect on the quality of the spiritual care for members of the churches. There were in the Korean Christian churches no persons trained in the Christian ministry until 1919. Those who had taken on the responsibility of church pastorate were people acquainted with some Bible lessons and written Korean language, hardly an acceptable qualification for the difficult task of caring for man's spiritual needs. Sometime in 1919 Min Ch'an-ho arrived in Honolulu after he had been ordained and admitted into the California Synod of the Presbyterian church. As an ordained man of God, however, Min did not live up to expectations commensurate with either the training that he had received or the ministerial ethics that he had pledged to uphold. According to Kingsley K. Lyu, Min began to perform the office of a bishop immediately after he had become pastor of the Korean Christian Church in Honolulu, and ordained men into the ministry of the Korean Christian churches. It is alleged by Lyu that Min had ordained more than ten of Rhee's supporters into Christian ministry by laying his hands on their heads. Therefore, when the Charter of the Central Korean Christian Church of Honolulu was obtained on December 9, 1924, the churches on the Islands of Oahu, Maui and Hawaii had pastors ordained by Min. [19]

The "ordained pastors" handpicked for their political and personal loyalty to Rhee soon began to turn churches into clubhouses for political lectures. Church services officiated by them usually began with a topic of political nature and ended with anouncement for political activities in connection with the Dongji-hoi or the Comrade Society, a political organization established on July 7, 1921 by Rhee to support his Korean national independence movement. It is said that during church services the pastors seldom neglected to praise Rhee who was remembered by them in their prayers. Those who neglected such decorum found themselves soon without a job. According to Lyu, a pastor, formerly of the Presbyterian faith, had accepted the pastorate at the Korean Christian Church, but he was soon relieved of his duty as he had forgotten to repeat the name of Rhee in his prayers. 20

It is not surprising, in retrospect, that the people ordained in such a hollow manner to hallow the Christian ministry confused personal loyalty to a political leader with services to mankind and an ideological message for an earthly kingdom with the universal message for the heavenly kingdom.

Conflicts and disputes did not end with the separation of the Rhee's followers from the Methodist church. The Korean Christian Church had a series of its own internal dissensions. The first occurred soon after Min's resignation in 1929. Min was forced to resign as he had been accused of misappropriating a $15,000 church building fund. His successor, Yi Yong-chik, was anxious to enforce the church regulations originally written by Syngman Rhee in the hope that the church would become a house of worship rather than a place for supporting Rhee's political activities. Soon the congregation was divided into two groups: one group supporting Yi and the other determined to oust him. Charges and counter-charges were made by both groups against each other, and thousands of dollars were spent as legal fees paid to prove the legitimate owner of the Korean Christian Church of Honolulu. Almost every Sunday the local police was called in to protect the church service officiated by Yi against the violence committed by the anti-Yi faction.

Another controversy occurred in the summer of 1946, when the pastor of the Korean Christian Church made an attempt to make the church a place for worship by separating politics from church affairs. With the approval of the church board, the pastor announced that the board and the pastor decided not to allow any person or group to use the church building for purposes other than church-related activities. This announcement touched off a series of verbal attacks against the pastor and members of the church board. A small number of church members led by a former assistant treasurer began to accuse the pastor of being anti-Rhee as he had failed to repeat the name of Rhee in his prayers. When the church board refused to recognize such a characterization of the pastor, the group made an attempt to take over the church administration by force on September 29, 1946. The controversy over which group was a real orthodox congregation of the Korean Christian Church was finally decided by the court that ordered the two groups to be united in October 1948. 21

Several churches of different denominations were established on the Mainland of the United States during the second period. As many Koreans began to move from the Hawaiian Islands to such metropolitan areas of the Mainland as Oakland, Los Angeles, Chicago, and New York, there was an increasing need to establish local churches. As early as June 1914, a small group of Korean residents in Oakland met at the residence of Moon Won-ch'il to conduct church services officiated by the Reverend Whang Sa-yong, who then worked for the Methodist Episcopal Church South. On August 10, 1917 the group moved its place of worship to the residence of Cho Sung-hak and invited Im Chong-ku, a student of Pacific School of Religion, Berkeley, California, to serve as evangelist for the group. After Im had become an ordained minister, the group negotiated with the Methodist Episcopal Mission for a place of worship. The mission sent the Reverend David, who appointed Im Chong-ku and No Sin-t'ae as evangelists for the church, which was officially established on March 2, 1929. In 1938 the group purchased a building located at Webster Street and dedicated it as a place of worship on December 20. In July, 1940 the congregation moved to another building located on Harrison Street in order to accommodate the increasing membership.

A group of Korean residents in New York negotiated with the Methodist Mission to establish a place for worship in February, 1923. The mission extended its helping hand by giving a large sum of money to purchase a building located on West 21st Street. The church building was dedicated on April 23. The congregation then moved to a larger building located on West 115th Street in order to accommodate an expanding church membership in October 1927. During the same year the Korean Methodist Church of Chicago, which had been established in July 1924, moved to a new building situated on Lake Park Avenue.

The Korean Presbyterian Church of Los Angeles developed a conflict soon after its establishment, and on October 14, 1924 a group of church members severed their relations from the church and established their own church known as the Free Church. The members of the Free Church sent their representatives on July 10, 1930 to the Methodist Episcopal Mission to ask for assistance in establishing a church. The mission sent the Reverend David, who officiated the establishment of the Korean Methodist Church of Los Angeles on October 16, 1930. Today, the church building is located on West 29th Street; it was dedicated on October 7, 1945.[22] Besides these Methodist churches established in major metropolitan areas, there was a Presbyterian church in Reedley, California which was organized in June 1936. Also a Christian church modeled after the Korean Christian Church of Honolulu was established by members of the Dongji-hoi in September 1936.

Compared with the second period in the history of the church in the Korean American community, which was replete with controversial disputes and conflicting interests, the third period between 1946 and 1967 was characterized by efforts on the part of the Ildae (first generation) to maintain the status quo, and by the attitude of indifference and rebellion on the part of Idae (second generation; Koreans born in America of immigrant parents) and Samdae (third generation; children of the second generation). A number of social, cultural and political factors seemed to have contributed to this intergenerational conflict.

First, the Ildae had seen their national sovereignity gradually eroded by the Japanese Empire prior to their departure for the Hawaiian Islands and the Mainland of the United States. After their arrival in America, most of them kept a burning patriotism for Korea intact, and they participated directly or indirectly in the effort to regain Korea's national independence. The Ildae as a whole had a political cause to fight and to live for through their life. However, to Idae and Samdae the political independence of Korea was more of an ideological rhetoric than a political imperative. After independence came to Korea in 1945, the issue of Korean national independence no longer served as a rallying point for Koreans in America.

Second, to Ildae the church was both a place of social interaction and cultural identification. After all, they spoke the same language and shared the same values and customs, and much of their unique cultural behavior was mutually reinforced in the social contacts provided by the church. Although the Idae had been under a strong cultural influence from the Ildae, they must have felt at times strange and somewhat alienated when they were taken to the church by their parents, who only spoke Korean to their contemporaries. So far as the Samdae was concerned, they could hardly identify themselves with the Ildae religiously, for they did not understand either their language or their culture. As pointed out by Kyung Sook Cho Gregor, the Idae "show a complete lack of interest in the matter of politics and religion." 23

Third, the Oriental Exclusion Law and the quota system in the American immigration policy from 1924 to 1968 24 prevented more Koreans from coming to the United States. Had they been allowed to enter, they would have provided their ethnic church with more vitality and spiritual leadership.

The fourth period in the history of the church in the Korean American community has begun with the new influx of immigrants into the United States, particularly into its large metropolitan areas, from Korea, which has sent more than 80,000 of its nationals since 1968. It is estimated that there are now as many as 50,000 Koreans in Los Angeles area alone, and more new arrivals are expected to join their countrymen in this area. This new wave of immigrants promises potential resources and leadership long needed for a revival of the ethnic church in the Korean American community. However, it also portends potential problems for the church. There are already some signs of stress and strain to which the church in the Korean American community has long been subjected. One of such signs is to be seen in the proliferation of churches founded on the bedrock of denominationalism. A number of historical and social forces seems responsible for the emergence of the denominational church within the Korean American community today. Due to an influx of new immigrants who arrive in the United States with their own religious preference, it is quite reasonable to expect them to look for the church of their choice or to establish their own denominational church. This seems to be a major cause for the proliferation of churches. For instance, there are today in the city of San Francisco nine churches attended almost exclusively by Koreans. Of these nine churches only two share the same denominational affiliation. These churches were originally established as denominational churches. 25

Other churches professing different brands of Christianity seem to have less than a clear philosophy for their denominational affiliation. Whether or not these churches have been established separately because of fine differences in the theological interpretation of the Bible is yet to be clarified. What seems clear to those who have carefully watched the painful and long metamorphosis of the Korean ethnic church is that the disputes over petty individual interests and honor rather than theological concerns have been a predominant reason for division within the church ever since its inception in the Korean American community. The recent dispute between two pastors of the Korean Missionary Church located at 11th and New Hampshire Streets in Los Angeles is a case in point. Apparently the church had been established under the leadership of the Reverend Ko Won-yong. Ko was elected chairman of the church board and the responsibility of running the church fell on his shoulder as chairman. Ko later invited one of his friends, the Reverend Chang Yun-song to take care of his congregation while he was away for his missionary duty. When he returned from his mission work to take on his position as pastor of the church he had helped to build, Chang refused to give in and claimed that the congregation had recognized him as a legitimate chairman of the church board. Chang continued to conduct church services and even refused to call upon Ko to officiate Sunday services. As Ko related in an interview with a newspaper reporter later, he felt that he was alienated from his own congregation. On one Sunday, Ko decided to lock the door of the church building where Chang was to hold his church service. Then he led a group of his sympathizers to the residence of a church elder for their own church service. Angered by Ko's action that had left approximately one hundred people stranded on the street, a group of four or five representatives from Chang's followers came to protest against Ko and disrupted the church service in progress. Irritated by their unexpected visitors, someone from Ko's group called in a local police force to intervene in the dispute. Today the congregation remains divided without a hope for reunification. 26

As has been observed, the new influx of a large number of Korean immigrants into the United States also promises a potential force for the growth and development of the Korean ethnic church. The number of churches is increasing by leaps and bounds. There are more than twenty churches in the Los Angeles area alone. And there are three Korean churches in the vicinity of Seattle, where they was not even a single church for Koreans prior to 1968.27

The sermons delivered from pulpits have improved in quality, and they have demonstrated deliberate efforts of pastors to interpret and teach the Bible without the attempts to influence the laymen's secular interests that had plagued the church in the Korean American community during the first and second periods of its history.

A critical examination of sermons frequently published in two leading Korean newspapers intended for those who know how to read the written Korean language offers a view of a broad spectrum of opinions and thoughts expressed by Korean clergymen. In his sermon 28 "Eternal Life or Eternal Death?" the Reverend Park Chong-gi, pastor of the San Diego Korean Church, expounded on the meaning of a scripture to be found in John 3:16. According to his interpretation, there are in the scripture four "major facts" to be studied by heart and accepted by faith so that their truth may be personalized. The first "fundamental and practical fact" to be derived from the scripture, Park continued, is that God loves man, that his love for man is unconditional, and that he loves man even before he becomes worthy of his love. God's love for man is the reason for man's salvation. The second "fact" is that God gave his only Son, who became his price for the redemption of man. The third "fact" is that man needs only to believe. The only condition for man's redemption is his faith in Christ Jesus as the Son of God. The fourth "fact" is that whoever believes shall not perish but have eternal life. This is the result of man's redemption.

One may argue with Park about some of the finer points of theological import of the often quoted scripture and even contend that he failed to provide his readers with criteria for what he called "facts." However, he has made an honest attempt to analyze the scripture, and he has presented to readers his own understanding of the true meaning of Christian love and redemption. This is more than what most of the early clergymen were willing or able to do, particularly during the first and second periods in the history of the Korean church.

Not all of the pastors seem satisfied with a strict clerical role of interpreting scriptures from the Bible and of teaching their meanings to increase the spiritual enrichment of their laymen. In an article published in the Miju dong-a (The Dong-A Daily in America) under the title "Freedom to the Oppressed," Kang Chin-sang, pastor of the San Diego Korean Federated Church, contends that the role of the Christian ministry should not be confined to preaching of the gospel for the heavenly kingdom. Characterizing as men of little faith and of self-deception those who comply with a strict interpretation of the Christion ministry, he challenged them to take on the responsibility of carrying the gospel to the poor in spirit and in their till, and of proclaiming freedom to the oppressed.[29] Obviously, Kang must have become irate over the news that the Seoul government incarcerated a group of young clergymen who had demanded a change to the constitution that would allow Koreans the freedom of speech, and of the press, the right to assembly, and other civil rights.

In spite of the conflicts and problems within the church already mentioned, it served a number of important needs of the Korean American community that would not otherwise have been met. It is unfortunate, retrospectively speeking, that the church had been swept into a vortex of political controversersies over the philosophical arguments and strategies for the Korean national independence movement during its embryonic stage. It is tragic particularly in view of the fact that so much of the energy and resources of the church was diverted to an unrealistic and naive notion that the leaders and their followers of the "Christian America," when sufficiently supplicated by their fellow Korean Christians, would assist them in their fight against Imperial Japan. The leaders of the Korean national independence movement were men who were largely ignorant of the American foreign policy toward Imperial Japan, particularly during the early period of their independence movement. They were also too ignorant of the dynamics of American domestic politics of accommodation to utilize it for their cause. Given the historical conditions under which the Korean independence movement was to be undertaken, however, the church played an active role in supporting propaganda and diplomatic efforts to restore Korea's independence.

The Korean independence movement was supported financially by a great number of small contributions made largely by Korean residents in Hawaiian Islands,[30] most of whom were members of local churches, particularly the Korean Christian churches. When the Korean Commission, established sometime in the autumn of 1919 in Washington D. C., issued bonds during the same year to generate the first $250,000 of the $5 million to be used in diplomatic and propaganda purposes, many Korean Christians purchased them. [31]

The church also played an active role in the educational and journalistic efforts to maintain and perpetuate Korean culture. Most of the Korean immigrants seemed to have sent their children to Korean language schools for practical as well as patriotic reasons. First of all, they wanted to bring up their children as Koreans. In order to achieve this goal in an alien culture, they needed an educational institution devoted to the teaching of Korean history, language, and culture. The church was chosen primarily for three reasons. First, there were already churches established in various work camps, and thus there was a basic organizational structure for the task. Second, most of the people qualified to teach children anything about Korea were pastors[32] who literate enough to instruct them. Third, due to lack of instructional materials, the Bible and Christian hymnbooks were used as textbooks.

Secondly, Korean immigrants established their language schools as a symbol of their national independence. There were already foreign language schools operated by Japanese and Chinese in the Islands and the Koreans were determined not to be surpassed in this crucial area of national culture. Thirdly, they saw an opportunity to put into practical use the Korean language to be learned by their children who were attending English-speaking schools. They hoped that their children would serve them as interpreters. [33] Various bulletins were published by a number of churches, and they were used both as newspapers and instructional materials, as they carried Bible lessons in Korean. One of the more important ones was published by the Korean Methodist Church of Honolulu. The church began its bulletin, the Honolulu Korean Church Bulletin, in November, 1904. The church continued to publish its bulletin until it was discontinued in October, 1940.

Available reports on the projects sponsored by the church in the Korean American community today seem to indicate that more emphasis is being given to recreational and social activities for group cohesion than to educational and political programs, though there are on the Mainland a few Korean language schools supported by the local churches. This is certainly in accord with the needs of the Korean ethnic community today, and it is highly desirable that the church detach itself from controversies over Korea's internal politics. There is, however, a vital need waiting to be filled in the Korean American community by either the church or other grass-roots social organizations. If Korean immigrants in America are to share fully with other Americans what their adopted country has to offer to its citizens, then they have to participate sooner or later in American domestic politics of accommodation, separatism, or radicalism. Whatever the choice of their political style may be, the Korean immigrants will soon be in need of an organizational base for their political participation in American politics. In the past, Irish and Italian Americans have used their ethnic affiliation with Catholicism rather effectively to gain their political power.[34] Whether or not Korean Americans will use their church as a political weapon remains to be seen.

Notes

1. Bernice Bong Hee Kim, "The Koreans in Hawaii," Social Science, Vol. IX, No. 4. October, 1934, p. 410. In her later work, "The Koreans in Hawaii," a master's thesis submitted to the University of Hawaii, she mentioned: "the Koreans were told that they were going to America, a Christian country, and that it would be the proper and advantageous thing to become Christians. All the young Koreans were eager to succeed in their venture, so one and all professed to become Christians." See "The Koreans in Hawaii," unpublished master's thesis (Sociology), University of Hawaii, 1937, 209 pp.

2. Fred Harvey Harrington, God, Mammon and the Japanese: Dr. Horace N. Allen and Korean-American Relations, 1884-1905. Madison, Wisconsin: University of Wisconsin Press, 1944, pp. 103-108.

3. Ibid., pp. 19-25.

4. Archives of Hawaii, Governors' Files, Carter-U.S. Depts. (October 1905 -- June 1907).

5. Tai Sung Lee, "The Story of Korean Immigration," The Korean Students' of Hawaii Yearbook, 1932 (The Korean Students' Alliance of Hawaii, Honolulu, Hawaii), p. 47.

6. The study on Deshler's biography is incomplete. According to Ch'oi Song-yon, the author of Kaehang kwa yangkwan yokchong, or Opening of Korea and History of Western-style Buildings, as reported by Yun Yo-jon, the author of Miju imin ch'ilsipnyon, or Seventy Years of Immigration in America, Deshler had joined the Orient Consolidated Mining Co. and lived in Chemulp'o, now Inch'on, with a Japanese woman. See Kyonghyang sinmun (Kyonghyang Daily), October 13, 1973.

7. Reports Public Instruction, December 31, 1910 -- December 1912, Honolulu, Department of Public Instruction, 1912, pp. 146-149.

8. George Heber Jones, "The Koreans in Hawaii," Korea Review, Vol. VI, No. 11, November 1906, p. 405.

9. Linda Shin in her study, "Koreans in America," published in Roots by Continental Graphics Company, Inc., in 1971, stated: "most of the emigrants who came to Hawaii before 1906 were relatively unorganized in traditional social groups." This seems to be an overstatement in view of the fact that Korean immigrants had maintained their traditional social organizations in Hawaii for the first few years. For a discussion of Korean social organizations in Hawaii during the first few years of their emigration, see Kingsley K. Lyu's "Korean National

Activities in Hawaii and America, 1901-1945," unpublished manuscript
in the possession of Professor Donald D. Johnson. The paper was submitted to Professor Johnson as a partial fulfillment of a research
course, History 300.

10. Jones, op. cit., p. 405.

11. Won-yong Kim, Chaemi Hanin osimnyonosa (A Fifty-Year History
of Koreans in America), Reedley, California: Charles Ho Kim, 1959,
p. 47.

12. Won-yong Kim, whose American name is Warren Kim, claims that
Wadman was relieved of his duty on June 1914. However, according to
a letter written by William Henry Fry, Wadman's immediate successor,
to L. E. Pinkham, governor of the Territory of Hawaii, dated July 27,
1915, Wadman was relieved of his duty on January 1, 1914.

13. Won-yong Kim, op. cit., pp. 42-43.

14. Miju dong-a (The Dong-a Daily in America), April 18, 1974, p. 1.

15. Kingsley K. Lyu, "Korean Nationalist Activities in Hawaii and Ameri-
1901-1945," unpublished manuscript in the possession of Professor
Donald D. Johnson, Graduate Division, University of Hawaii, 1950,
pp. 52-53. It should be pointed out that Yang Yu-ch'an was later appointed by Sygman Rhee as Korean ambassador to the United States,
when Rhee became the first president of the Republic of Korea.

16. The Honolulu Advertiser, July 3, 1915, p. 10.

17. Kingsley K. Lu, Op. cit., p. 64.

18. Ibid., p. 68.

19. Ibid., p. 71.

20. Ibid., p. 75.

21. Ibid., p. 76.

22. Kyung Lee, "Settlement Patterns of Los Angeles Koreans," unpublished master's thesis, University of California, Los Angeles, 1969,
p. 35.

23. Kyong Sook Cho Gregor, "Korean Immigrants in Gresham, Oregon:
Community Life and Social Adjustment," unpublished master's thesis,
University of Oregon, 1963, p. 54.

24. Although the Act of October 3, 1965 (P.L. 89-236) repealed the
national origin quota system established in 1924, the act included a

three-year phase-out period.

25. Miju dong-a (The Dong-A Daily in America), April 4, 1974, p. 2.

26. Miguk sosik (The American News), February 26, 1973, p. 1.

27. Miguk sosik (The American News), April 23, 1974, p. 1.

28. Miju dong-a (The Dong-A Daily in America), March 28, 1974, p. 2.

29. Miju dong-a (The Dong-A Daily in America), April 18, 1974, p. 2.

30. A careful count of the number of people who promised to make a contribution, as reported in the Korean Pacific Weekly, an official bulletin published by the Dongji-Hoi, indicates that a total of sixty-nine persons promised a sum of $1,026. This is less than $15 per person. See Korean Pacific Weekly, Series 28, Vol. 12, No. 482, June 14, 1941, p. 19.

31. Won-yong Kim, Op. cit., p. 379.

32. Helen Lewis Givens, "The Korean Community in Los Angeles," unpublished master's thesis, University of Southern California, 1939, p. 38.

33. Kingsley K. Lyu, Op. cit., p. 33.

34. Edgar Litt, Ethnic Politics in America, Glenview, Illinois: Scott, Foresman and Company, 1970, pp. 60-80.

BIBLIOGRAPHY OF SELECTED REFERENCES

I. General Bibliographies

Gardner, Arthur L. The Koreans in Hawaii: An Annotated Bibliography
Honolulu, Hawaii: Social Science Research Institute, University
of Hawaii, 1970. 83 pp.

II. Books in Korean

Chae-Mi Hanjok yonhap wiwon-hoi (The United Korean Committee in
America), ed., Haebang Choson (Liberated Korea). Los Angeles,
1948. 226 pp.

Kim, Won-yong. Chae-Mi Hanin osimnyonsa (A Fifty Year History of
the Koreans in the United States). Reedley, California: Charles
Ho Kim, 1959. 514 pp.

Koh, Sung-che. Han'guk iminsa yon-gu (A Study of the History of Korean
Emigration). Seoul, 1973. 375 pp.

Noh, Jae-yon. Chae-Mi Hanin saryak, Vol. I (A Short History of Koreans
in America). Los Angeles, 1951. 180 pp.

_____. Chae-Mi Hanin saryak, Vol. II (A Short History of Koreans
in America). Los Angeles, 1963. 175 pp.

Suh, Kwang-woon. Miju Hanin ch'ilsimnyonsa (A Seventy Year History
of Koreans in America). Seoul, 1973. 185 pp.

III. Articles in Korean

Chong, Du-ok. "Chae-Mi Hanjok tongnip undong silgi" (A Record of the
Independence Activities of the Koreans in the United States), The
Han'guk ilbo, February 28, 1961 -- March 3, 1961.

Sin, Hung-wu. "Miju ui p'alch'on dongp'o kunhwang" (The Present
Situation of Our Eight Thousand Countrymen in the United States),
in P'yongwha wa chayu (Peace and Freedom), Kim Tong-whan, ed.,
pp. 287-290. Seoul, 1932.

Yun, Yo-chon. "Miju imin ch'ilsimnyon" (Seventy years of Emigration to
America), Kyonghyang sinmun, October 6, 1973 -- December 27,
1973.

IV. Books in English

Hawaii Korean Golden Jubilee Committee. Fifty Years of Progress:

Hawaii Korean Golden Jubilee Celebration. Honolulu, 1953. 40 pp.

Koh, Kwang-lim and Hesung C. Koh, ed. Koreans and Korean-Americans in the United States: A Summary of Three Conference Proceedings. New Haven: East Rock Press, Inc., 1974. 137 pp.

V. Articles in English

Appenzeller, Alice R. "A Generation of Koreans in Hawaii," Paradise of the Pacific, Vol. LVI, No. 12, (December 1944), pp. 81-83.

Dunn, J. Kyuang. "Progress of Koreans in Hawaii," Paradise of the Pacific, Vol. LVIII, No. 12, (December 1946), pp. 90-91.

Handley, Katherine N. "Our Standards Are Different," in Four Case Studies in Hawaii: Intercultural problems and the Practice of Social Work, Honolulu: University of Hawaii Press, 1961, pp. 52-57.

Hulbert, Homer B. "The Koreans in Hawaii," Korea Review, Vol. V., No. 11, (November 1905), pp. 411-413.

Jhung, Walter. "Korean Independence Activities of Overseas Koreans," Korean Survey, Vol. 1, No. 4, (December 1952), pp. 7-10.

Jones, George Heber. "Koreans Abroad," Korea Review, Vol. VI, No. 12, (December 1906), pp. 446-451.

——————. "The Koreans in Hawaii," Korea Review, Vol. VI, No. 11, (November 1906), pp. 401-406.

Kang, Donald. "The Koreans in Hawaii," New Pacific, Vol. 11, No. 11, (November 1944), pp. 4-5.

Kim, Bernice Bong Hee. "The Koreans in Hawaii," Social Science, Vol. IX, No. 4, (October 1934), pp. 409-413.

Kim, Hyung-chan. "Korean Emigrants to the U.S.A., 1959-1969," Korea Journal, Vol. XI, No. 9, (September 1971), pp. 16-24, 31.

——————. "Some Aspects of Social Demography of Korean Americans," International Migration Review, Vol. VIII, Number 1 (Spring 1974), pp. 23-42.

"A Korean Appeal to America," The Nation, Vol. 108, No. 2807, (April 19, 1919), pp. 638-639.

"Koreans Celebrate March 1st," Korea Review, Vol. IV, No. 2, (April 1922), pp. 15-16.

Lee, Tai Sung. "The Story of Korean Immigration," The Korean Students' of Hawaii Yearbook, 1932, pp. 47-49.

Lind, Andrew W. "Hawaii's Koreans -- Some Basic Considerations," Bohk Dohng, Vol. 1, No. 4, (April 29, 1956), pp. 3-4.

Moore, S. F. "One Night with the Koreans in Hawaii," Korea Review, Vol. III, No. 12, (December 1903), pp. 529-532.

Pang, Morris. "A Korean Immigrant," Social Forces in Hawaii, Vol. XIII, (1949), pp. 19-24.

Shin, Linda. "Koreans in America," in Roots, published by Continental Graphics Incorp., 1971, pp. 200-206.

Shular, Helen. "Halmunee with a Korean Accent," Paradise of the Pacific, Vol. LXIX, No. 3, (March 1957), pp. 22-24.

VI. Unpublished Materials

Church, Deborah. "Korean Emigration to Hawaii: An Aspect of U.S. -- Japanese Relations," unpublished study, University of Hawaii, 1971, 50 pp.

Eubark, Lauriel E. "The Effects of the First Six Months of World War II on the Attitudes of Koreans and Filipinos toward the Japanese in Hawaii," master's thesis, University of Hawaii, 1943. 190 pp.

Givens, Helen Lewis. "The Korean Community in Los Angeles County," master's thesis, University of Southern California, 1939, 85 pp.

Gregor, Kyung Sook Cho, "Korean Immigrants in Gresham, Oregon: Community Life and Social Adjustment," master's thesis, University of Oregon, 1963, 93 pp.

Kim, Bernice Bong Hee. "The Koreans in Hawaii," master's thesis, University of Hawaii, 1937. 209 pp.

Lee, Kyung. "Settlement Patterns of Los Angeles Koreans," master's thesis, University of California at Los Angeles, 1969. 81 pp.

Lyu, Kingsley K. "Korean Nationalist Activities in Hawaii and America, 1901-1945," unpublished study, University of Hawaii, 1950. 153 pp.

Yoo, Jai-kun. "The Koreans in the United States: A Seattle Study," unpublished study by the Korean Community Survey Project, 1973. 110 pp.